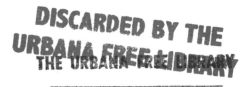
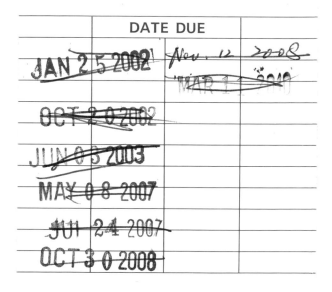

Effective Letters for Every Occasion

Effective Letters for Every Occasion

Casey Fitts Hawley

BARRON'S

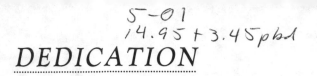

DEDICATION

To my son, Houston Hawley. Your goodness is an inspiration to me.
Thank you for coming into the world as such a wonderful person.
You make life fun, rich, and full of opportunities to write notes!

All inquiries should be addressed to:
Barron's Educational Series, Inc.
250 Wireless Boulevard
Hauppauge, New York 11788
http://www.barronseduc.com

International Standard Book No.: 0-7641-1213-9

Library of Congress Catalog Card No.: 99-63087

Printed in the United States of America
9 8 7 6 5 4 3 2 1

ACKNOWLEDGMENTS

Sue Bentley,
President, Junior League of Cobb County, 1998–1999; Controller,
Scottish Rite Hospital; Bible Study Fellowship Leader.

Janel Wiles,
Board member, Cobb Family Resources; hostess and wife of State
Representative John Wiles; Francophile; law partner.

Barbara Taylor,
Curator, Menaboni Exhibit, Marietta Cobb Museum of Art; guest
instructor—The Art Place; Chattahoochee Nature Center gala coordinator.

Luanne Bentley,
Board member, Georgia Ballet; insurance executive; room mother;
Book Fair Chairman; producer of exquisite little events.

Keli Stowell,
Word processing expert; creator of this book's templates; mom;
active church and school volunteer.

Jan Julian,
Sales representative; church volunteer; sports enthusiast; bon vivant;
good deed doer; mother, daughter, wife, and friend.

Trisha White,
Owner, Anna Ball White's Boutique; leading national interior designer;
executive hostess (Lookout Mountain, New York, Atlanta, etc.).

Sherry Gentry,
Suntrust bank executive, corporate wizard, hostess of Georgia's
best big parties, Vacation Bible School Coordinator.

From each of you, I have learned so much. By showing me how you communicate, you have taught me what excellent communication is. You speak and write with grace and style and great kindness. You always know the most appropriate things to say and choose the most perfect words to express your thoughts. I have learned that you put much thought into some letters that require tact or compassion or sensitivity. You never fail to find just the right approach to any letter or note. This book was easy for me because I had you, my dear friends, for such wonderful models.

Thank you, Casey

CONTENTS

CHAPTER

1

HOW TO WRITE TODAY'S LETTERS

Introduction

•

Letter Writing: A New Frontier

•

Top Ten Reasons to Write Personal Letters

INTRODUCTION

Y ou are about to discover a way of writing letters that will make your letters highly effective, truly memorable, and distinctively personal. When your friends or associates receive a letter from you, adapted from the samples in this book, you can expect to receive the responses you want.

- Are you writing to complain about poor service in a restaurant? Your letter (as adapted from this book) will get the manager's attention and respect. Expect an offer of a free dinner along with an apology.

- Is your letter a tender one, expressing your affection for an old friend? Expect to touch that person's heart as you never have before. These letters show you an easy way to put into words, in a highly personal way, the feelings and ideas you may have struggled to express.

- Is your letter a simple dinner invitation to a colleague? This book will show you how to do it right, with no mix-ups or embarrassing mistakes.

Almost any situation you can think of can be written about using one of the templates (form letters) in this book. Why is this book so effective? Easy, fill-in-the-blank letters are given to you. You simply add the details that relate to your reader and your life. These letters practically write themselves. Just choose the names and items that apply to your letter, fill in the blanks, sign it, and mail it! Or you may write your own highly original letter using the template as a basis.

Language

The simple, direct language used by real people when they personally write letters is used in this book. The TIPS and how-tos are written in a real-world, conversational style, and so are the letters. The person-to-person style makes learning to write personal letters easy and accessible—even for those who think they are poor writers.

The letters are written in authentic, conversational style because confident people write their personal letters in this simple direct language. *These letters do not sound as if they were copied from a book!*

Freedom of Choice

You make the choices that make these letters sound like you. You choose certain words to fill in the blanks. Those words reflect your personality and sentiments. The letters reflect who you are and how you feel about the subject of your letter.

Tips & How-Tos

Every chapter begins with the best available inside information about how to write a particular type of letter: an apology, a thank-you note, a letter of complaint, or whatever you need. These TIPS help you write a letter that achieves your goal.

- Do you want someone to know how genuinely you appreciated a unique and thoughtful gift? Chapter Three, "Friendship," will tell you the techniques that will set your thank-you note apart from all the rest. When your reader receives her note, she will know how authentic your appreciation is.

- Do you want to say something special to a bereaved friend? The TIPS will give you just the right wording to express your condolences in a unique and caring way.

- Do you want to express your support or admiration for your minister or state representative? In Chapter Nine, "Corresponding with Professional People," you will find just the right words to praise a job well done, request services, or voice a complaint. At the same time, you will be enhancing your personal credibility by writing such an excellent letter. The how-tos and samples assure that your letter is among the best these professionals will ever receive.

You are encouraged to experiment with the samples and the word lists. As you borrow from these excellent prewritten letters, your confidence will grow. The lists of words given to you will stimulate your imagination. You will soon be adding great lines of your own. Be assured, however, that these letters are winning and effective even if you simply fill in the blanks and mail them out.

People Love Letters

People love to receive letters. Take the very same conversation that you would have had in a phone call, package the conversation as a letter, and presto! You have given someone the gift of a letter.

Do you remember a time that it warmed your heart, excited you, or made you feel less empty because you found a letter in your mailbox? It's so easy to give someone that warm feeling by simply putting your thoughts on paper and mailing them.

Easy Letters Take Little Time

People appreciate almost any letter, long or short. You'd be surprised how much they value your efforts. The purpose of this book is to give you some tools so you can write great letters in minutes. The templates and examples will give you the means to write meaningful, polished, personal letters with almost no effort.

LETTER WRITING:
A NEW FRONTIER

People are returning to writing letters. Why? Many reasons are pushing us to write letters to friends, acquaintances, and relatives.

The main reason letter writing is returning is that we are busy. A working mom returns home at 5:30 P.M. and puts her children to bed at 8:30 P.M. after preparing their dinner. She does not want to give up one of these precious hours to the telephone. When this woman has a quiet moment, it's likely to be very late at night or very early in the morning. Both times are wrong for a phone call but just right for writing a quick note to a friend.

A busy executive may find he has neglected to call an elderly relative. The rush and pressure of a typical day does not allow time for tasks that are not urgent or compelling. On a plane ride home from a meeting, the executive writes a brief newsy letter that his relative cherishes and rereads for weeks afterwards. A need is met. A letter, as usual, is deeply appreciated.

TOP TEN REASONS
TO WRITE PERSONAL
LETTERS

1. A personal letter says to the recipient, "You are special, and I took my time to acknowledge how special you are." A phone call just doesn't make a person feel singled out and pampered the way a personal letter does.

2. Letters document the important and special moments in our lives: weddings, births, graduations, new careers, losses, special weekends, dinner with friends, and much, much more. In our busy lives, letters are a wonderful way to chronicle our lives and our personal histories as we go along. Create and cherish memories in a permanent way: Write a letter.

3. Writing letters is an efficient use of our time. Does that surprise you? I often hear people say, "I don't have time to write." These same people waste hours on the telephone in conversations they wish they could cut short. Letters put you in charge of the time you are willing to invest. Once you learn the system to kick out a great letter in minutes (as taught in this book), you can communicate with lots of friends or relatives and invest a fraction of the time.

4. Letters give you the time, peace, and quiet to formulate what you want to say, choosing exactly the right words. Sometimes, live conversations don't always allow us this luxury; they move too quickly. Who hasn't said something spontaneously in conversation that we wished we could erase or rephrase? That's not possible with conversation, but it is in a letter. You can strike through and start again if you mistakenly choose an offensive or emotionally charged word. Conversation isn't that forgiving.

5. Letters give information faster, clearer, and better. Fewer misunderstandings occur when you put invitations and plans in writing. Do you want Suzy to show up at 7:00 P.M., Saturday, April 16 for a dinner? Better put it in a letter. Otherwise, Suzy may be your surprise dinner guest on April 9!

6. A letter fills up loneliness or emptiness much longer than a conversation does. A letter or invitation can be pulled out, reread, savored, and enjoyed over and over again. It's not unusual to see a special letter saved in a person's desk drawer or on a table or cabinet. Just the sight of it can create a warm spot in a heart that is feeling empty.

7. As you write, you problem solve. Putting your thoughts down on paper helps you clarify and organize. Writing helps focus you, so

you can make a better decision. Forcing yourself to write out your feelings and thoughts helps you to articulate—even to yourself— exactly what you feel and what you don't. Many people write "therapeutic" letters that they have no intention of sending. Why? The very process of writing a letter to a friend or relative is cathartic and liberating. These letters may never be mailed, but they help the writer acknowledge emotions and organize thoughts.

8. An even more serious reason to write letters is that some people view your not writing as an intentional insult. Some segments of society can become extremely hurt or mortally offended if you do not write the expected conventional letters. These traditionalists may not only view you as uncouth; they may honestly believe that you have intentionally slighted them by failing to write letters about changes in your life. For example, many people expect a letter informing them of deaths, births, weddings, and other major life changes. If you don't meet these "responsibilities," some may feel hurt and offended.

   There is a segment of our population that still believes social correspondence is not optional—it's an obligation. Cultural norms for some parts of our society dictate that you are required to write thank-you notes and to extend invitations in writing. If you do not fulfill these expectations, you are viewed as ignorant, rude, uncouth, and crass.

9. Letters are great documentation. We often think that we will remember events, places, and people forever. As life goes on, however, we are amazed to find that we have forgotten the name of the son of our old next-door neighbor in a neighborhood we lived in years ago. If you choose to save letters you will be surprised at how many memories they will bring back, memories you can review before visits, reunions, and vacations.

10. A letter is a bond between two people. We telephone lots of people. To how many people do we write? When a new friend receives a letter, it raises that friendship to a whole new level. It's the beginning of a bonding process, and it's a nice way to start.

CHAPTER

2

HOW TO USE THIS BOOK

How This Book Works

•

Writing in Today's Style

•

Why are Today's Letters Shorter?

HOW THIS BOOK WORKS

Y ou will be amazed at the highly personalized and warm letters you can create in minutes from the sample letters in this book.

When you see the samples, you might think that they look a bit unusual. These examples are templates. A template is a basic form that you can change and adapt to create many different letters. By making a few changes to the basic template letter, you can create a letter tailored to your reader, event, and circumstances.

Results

By using the templates, you'll have dynamic, personal-sounding letters. You can send out your letter, confident that it is well thought out and appropriate.

Easy

The basic letter is completely written, formatted, and polished for you. All you need to do is insert the names of your recipients or the description of your gift, or event, or other details. In many cases, you have lists of words to choose from to help you fill in the blanks. How easy can letter writing get?

Fast

You no longer have to labor over what to say. Just fill in the blanks. You will finish most letters in five minutes or less. If you want to add your own sentences and creative touches, you will make the letter even better!

How Do The Templates Work?

Every letter is prewritten for you. There are blanks for you to fill in that describe your particular situation, person, or event.

For example, suppose you are writing a thank-you letter for a gift. The letter has already been written for you. You insert the name of your gift: a vase, a new putter, a box of chocolates. You also insert a word describing that gift. The descriptive word can easily be chosen from the list on page 22. Examples of describing words include exotic, delicate, updated, state-of-the-art, richly detailed, technically perfect, gracious, fine, and gourmet.

By simply filling in the blanks, you will have a letter that gratifies your reader. Your reader sees a letter with all of the following qualities and more:

- Highly personalized
- Well written
- Unique
- Pleasant and warm

After you begin using these letters with people you know, expect to hear comments like these from your friends and acquaintances:

- "What a great letter!"
- "That was an especially nice letter, not just routine."
- "Thank you. Your letter really made me feel special."

Many letters in the book are also useful for your personal business. These letters will get the job done effectively—whatever it is.

Formatting Letters Correctly

You may wish to use the book's word lists in order to create your own highly original letter. If so, check out Chapter Thirteen, "Formatting Personal Letters." There you will find TIPS and examples that will help you produce a polished letter that meets today's standards.

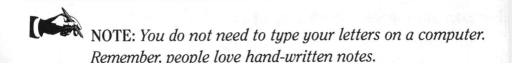

NOTE: *You do not need to type your letters on a computer. Remember, people love hand-written notes.*

WRITING IN TODAY'S STYLE

Personal letters **look** different today and the writing style has definitely changed. In the last ten years we have seen a dramatic change in the sentence structure, format, and tone of personal letters.

Today's style is brief and to the point. Both writers and readers are busy people—pushed for time. If you are writing a letter to a friend who has limited time, your friend's delight is not diminished because your letter is brief. It's truly the thought that counts.

This book employs the higher energy and somewhat briefer style of the new millennium. Although this style is not very formal, people respond to it positively. Your letters will have the ring of a warm and sincere conversation.

WHY ARE TODAY'S LETTERS SHORTER?

E-mail

The influence of E-mail can't be discounted when we see how letters are getting shorter and shorter. E-mail taught a whole generation of non-letter writers some important lessons:

- You can communicate effectively in a short document.

- Readers are gratified to be thought of and written to—even if only a few lines. A letter still says, "I cared enough to write," or "I'm thinking of you."

- E-mail freed many people from their hang-ups and self-consciousness about grammar and writing style. For some reason, people didn't feel that they had to punctuate and proofread E-mail. Eliminating this liberated more people to write. As a result, many people discovered the joy of corresponding with friends and family. Of course, we want our letters to be grammatically and mechanically correct. Still, we have learned that, to most readers, accuracy is not nearly as important as the fact that we took the time to write.

Women's Changing Lives

One hundred years ago, social correspondence was as vital a skill to a woman as cooking or sewing. When few people had telephones, letter writing was a necessity. Like many chores, writing letters was the wife's responsibility. She had enough time for this because, naturally, she did not work outside the home.

My, how times have changed. Working moms, wives, and single women now have little time for letter writing of the old-fashioned variety. If a woman gets five minutes to communicate with a friend, she is much more likely to pick up a phone and make a quick call. If she writes a letter, it's probably dashed off in a hurry, so it's brief. One of the purposes of this book is to help a busy person use those same five minutes to turn out a dynamite letter.

Busy People—Busy Lives—Fast-Track Employees

Women are not the only ones feeling the time crunch. Male executives and other business professionals find that companies are demanding more and more hours. Simultaneously, business people are urged to network and follow up with other professionals they meet at civic and charitable events. This type of follow up, if done well, is done with a letter. Sadly, employees on the fast track to success find out they failed to learn one important skill: how to write a credible and engaging personal letter. This book does that for you. You only have to insert the words that describe the events, organizations, and other details from your life.

Media Influence

Today's magazines aim for a very elementary reading level—usually sixth to ninth grade. Need we even mention the low standards for comprehension set by television? Such low expectations have influenced us dramatically as readers. We expect our reading material to be written in short sentences using easy words. When

I do seminars around the country about writing, I start by asking what people read first in their mail. They mention many things. The one thing that every group in every state says, however, is that they read the short, easy things first. You may not like this revelation, but it's true. Our taste in letters has changed.

How Has Sentence Structure Changed?

Media's other influences include two important changes that affect our letters greatly:

1. Media has taught people to receive information in short, simple bits or bytes. Sentences in today's letters should therefore be simpler and shorter. The rule today is to put in one idea per sentence.

   Do you remember how your high school English teachers taught you to move from simple to complex sentences? Do you remember when you finally arrived at the pinnacle—writing in compound-complex sentences? This is a skill you'll rarely need today. Even our more educated readers prefer simpler sentences. A good letter writer will mix short and long sentences.

2. The media has also raised our expectations of how a document should look. Although you probably won't include graphics in a personal letter, your reader does expect correspondence to look sharp. It has also become acceptable to put key information in bulleted form—almost like a mini-poster. Using bullets is an excellent way to cut down on confusion and misunderstandings. For example, if you are writing a letter of invitation, put the following in bulleted form:

   - What: Event
   - When: Time and Date
   - Where: Address

Your Computer Can Help Teach You to Write in Today's Style

Although they still love to receive hand-written notes, more and more people are typing personal letters on their computers. One of the most popular writing tools of the decade has been word processing software. Most packages include a tool to critique our writing. These tools tell us how readable and acceptable our document will be to our reader. Virtually all word processing packages give documents a score, usually interpreted as the grade level of our document. For example, we may write a letter on our computer. The writing tool evaluates the letter and tells us the letter is written at an eighth-grade level. Now, look at your "Help" or information file. This file tells you what a score means. Is it a good or bad score? In almost every case, letters written at the sixth-grade to ninth-grade levels are labeled "good." Letters written at much higher grade levels have labels such as "bad," "unreadable," or "too complex." These scores are based on tests and surveys of thousands of readers. They tell us that today's reader wants simplicity.

How Can I Personalize My Letters?

You can make your reader feel that even a short letter was composed very personally for him/her. How is that possible if you are working from a template or form letter? Here are four easy steps to a personal tone:

1. Use first- and second-person pronouns: I, we, our, us, you, your, yours. Write the way you talk. Use a few contractions: let's, can't, we're. Avoid awkward formal sentences.

2. Ask a question or two. Examples: How's fatherhood? Did you ever get the bass boat you wanted?

3. Choose from the many lists of words this book offers. On pages 22 to 24, 34, and 35 you will find many choices of words to make your letters unique.

4. Personalize by finding the most descriptive words. Better yet, use these word lists to jog your imagination. Come up with your own words to insert.

Using the techniques above will give your letter a remarkably personal tone.

CHAPTER

3

FRIENDSHIP

TIPS: How to Write a Memorable Thank-You Note

•

Why Are Notes and Personal Letters Important?

•

What Does a Good Note Require?

•

Thank-You Notes

•

Notes for All Occasions

- How do I write a note that sounds personal and unique to my reader?

- How can I turn out a great note in minutes instead of agonizing over what to say?

- How do I convey the sincerity of my appreciation or friendship instead of sounding trite?

TIPS: HOW TO WRITE A MEMORABLE THANK-YOU NOTE

One of the most powerful documents in the world is the thank-you note. Almost universally, however, people have difficulty writing these short but meaningful notes.

On a personal level, thank-you notes bond us more closely to the giver. The note is as much an acknowledgment of the giver as of the gift. This acknowledgment can help cement an existing friendship or warm a growing relationship.

In business, the thank-you note is a must. Corporate etiquette demands that career-minded people write notes of thanks, not only for gifts but for invitations, lunches, and any help they receive on their way up the ladder.

Your first challenge is to personalize the note so that the recipient feels all the warmth of your sincere appreciation. The second challenge is to find a shortcut to personalizing so that you can write these notes in minutes rather than hours.

Instant Personalization
of Thank-You Notes

You have two shortcuts to personalizing the thank-you note.

- Use one word in the first sentence to describe the gift.
- Use one word in the first sentence to describe the giver.

The first sentence of a note tells the reader if you really value the gift (or event) or if this is just a perfunctory, write-it-'cause-you-have-to note. Just one word, personally chosen by you, can set your note apart from the meaningless, bland notes sent by most others.

Your reader really doesn't mind whether you use your one unique word to describe the gift or the giver. Gratification is what thank-you notes are all about. On the following pages are a few of the many choices of words to describe gifts and givers. Who knows? You may find this so easy you will choose one from each list!

Describing Words—Gifts/Events

advanced	froo-froo	rich
arresting	fun	safe
art	glossy	secure
attractively presented	gold	shimmering
beautifully planned	gossamer	shiny
best	gripping	silk
best on the market	handmade	silver
casual	homemade	sophisticated
ceramic	inspiring	spectacular
cherished	investment quality	sporty
china	invigorating	striking
choice	Irish linen	sturdy
classic	jeweled	subdued
colorful	lasting	sumptuous
convenient	leather	symmetry
cool	luxurious	tart
cotton	luxury	tasteful
current	manly	tasty
cutting edge	many features	technology
decadent	masculine	timeless
dependable	needed	timely
discovery	new version	treat
durable	newly released	useful
efficient	nicely appointed	valuable
elegant	not fussy	valued
enduring	opportunity	vastly improved
enjoyable	perfectly proportioned	warm
ergonomic	playful	well designed
exceptional	pleasant	well engineered
exciting	pottery	well made
exclusive	premium	well organized
feminine	proposal	whimsical
finely designed	proven	wise
finely detailed	prudent	wonderful
finely executed	relaxed	world class
free	reliable	woven

Nouns for Naming Gifts

a great gift	contribution	keepsake
addition	encouragement	memorable one
asset	excellent example of ___	rarity
choice addition	fine piece of equipment	treasure
collector's item	heirloom	upgrade

What Does the Gift Do?

Your gift . . .

- Will be used frequently because _____

- Completes my (apartment, set, table setting, outfit, morning routine, dream, etc.)

- Accentuates _____

- Fulfills my wish/need for _____

- Will help me _____

- Will be more valuable to me each year

- Is an important addition to my collection, study, etc.

NOTE: *If the brand name is a good one, mention it. Examples: Godiva chocolate · Rolex watches · Rolls Royce · Craftsman tools · Waterford crystal · Mont Blanc pen · Givenchy or other designers*

Describing Words—Givers/Hosts

accomplished	forward thinking	risk taking
artistic	fun	self-sacrificing
athletic	giving	sensitive
aware	healthy	sportsminded
caring	helpful	tasteful
creative	indulgent	thoughtful
discerning	multidimensional	visual
discriminating	nurturing	whimsical
dramatic	observant	wise
far thinking	on the forefront	extraordinaire
financial savvy	playful	world class

Nouns That Refer to Giver

connoisseur	hero	model
craftsman	host	prolific reader
culinary expert	initiator	provider of good things
entrepreneur	investor	visionary
futurist	literary	veteran

Etceteras

You . . .

- Are a good cook, business person, money manager, dad, technophile, planner;

- Have excellent taste, an eye for beautiful things, just the right touch, my interests at heart;

- Give richly of your time, talent, resources, broad network, etc.;

- Think of others' needs, serve others, notice the needs of others.

How to Use Word Lists

These word lists are just the beginning. After you go through the lists, other unique and perfectly appropriate words will come to you. If you see a word that is almost perfect, look it up in your thesaurus. If you have a computer, it probably has a thesaurus in its word processing package. The thesaurus will suggest even more words to you. With all these choices, odds are you'll find just the right word to say to your special reader.

Don't forget to use a word about the gift or the giver in the very first sentence!

WHY ARE NOTES AND PERSONAL LETTERS IMPORTANT?

Notes are highly valued and even expected by some people. You may not be aware of how many people anxiously look for a note following an event or after giving a gift. If you don't find these letters important, you may mistakenly think that others feel as you do. Nothing could be further from the truth. Many of our friends and business associates consider a good thank-you note a basic courtesy.

Unfortunately, many people do not write good notes. A note does not generate the goodwill desired if it is poorly or hastily executed. Here are some pet peeves of those who receive such notes.

- Notes are dashed off so hastily that the lack of care is obvious.

- The writer misspells the receiver's name or other names in the note. How personal is that?

- The wording reflects no thought or sincerity. One note I read said, "Thank you for the portfolio. It was nice." The receiver felt that only minimum attention was given to his gift, and he was right!

WHAT DOES A GOOD NOTE REQUIRE?

Correctness

You should check the spelling of names, proofread text, and be accurate about details.

Content

Your content should be personalized and professional. If a friend/client/co-worker spent time selecting a gift or preparing for an event for you, you should spend a few minutes choosing words to reflect his or her thoughtfulness. What was unique about the gift or experience? What was particularly well done? What made it especially helpful or attractive to you personally? Write about one or more of these things.

Presentation

The paper you use does not need to be expensive, but it should be in good taste. Plain white or cream is always safe, but other simple conservative looks may work well too. If you write the note by hand, pay attention to neatness. To some people, a sloppy note says, "I'm just doing this because I have to and I really don't care." That may not be what you feel, but it's the message you're sending.

THANK-YOU NOTES

Most of the samples on the following pages are in note form. Even in the business world, our readers find short notes acceptable and welcome. Only the most formal business relationships require a letter. In earlier days, people always hand-wrote personal letters and notes, but today many type them.

Quick and easy to write, the following note is sure to win friends and influence people! You have been given a template (a fill-in-the-blank form) to help you. To create a winning note, just write words that describe your gift or event in the spaces.

You can also use the template to get a few ideas and create your own letter. Create thousands of personalized thank-you letters and notes from this same template. You will find examples of thank-you notes using the template on pages 28–33.

The Five-Minute Killer Thank-You Note

Your <u>gift/invitation/dinner meeter</u> is so <u>gift word, page 22</u>.
(colorful, much needed)

I really <u>choose a verb</u>
(like/need/wanted/looked forward to/enjoyed/am excited about/was fascinated by/savored the food and company)

<u>gift/event/dish</u>.   A good <u>name the gift or event</u> is
(a new tennis racquet/a new   *(tennis racquet/briefcase/*
briefcase/the dinner/the banquet)   *dinner party/corporate event)*

<u>insert a phrase or noun</u> and is something I value. I look forward to
(a rarity/a great gift for me/always nice)

<u>insert a phrase below or your own</u>.
(using it/fishing with it/serving with it/hanging it/decorating my den with it/future meetings/next year's banquet/our appointment next week/seeing you in October/ doing this again soon/reciprocating/seeing you soon/more occasions like this/ returning the invitation/having you over, too)

For a longer letter:

Thank you again for a(n) <u>describe the experience</u> <u>event/gift</u>.
(exceptional/   *(evening/*
thoughtful/great)   *meeting/gift)*

How Do I Use the Template for a Thank-You Note?

Your gift is so sporty and well designed. I really needed it. A good tennis racquet is valuable to me. I look forward to serving with it.

Thank you again for an exceptional gift.

....

NOTE: *Do you see how the blanks of the template have been filled in by the writer of the note above?*

How Do I Use the Template for an Event?

Your dinner party was so beautifully planned and attractively presented. I really savored the food and the company. A good dinner party is a rarity. I look forward to returning the invitation soon.

Thank you again for an exceptional evening.

 NOTE: *This note is from the same template as the one on page 28. The second writer simply chose different words to fill in the blanks.*

That Style Doesn't Sound Like Me—How Can I Make the Note Sound as if I Wrote It?

You have two choices.

Option 1: Simply changing the words in the blanks makes the note radically different. The words you put in the blanks reflect your personality and personal style. Below is the same note written using more casual words. Do you see how the style of the note changes completely?

Your <u>Wednesday night supper</u> was so much <u>fun</u> and <u>relaxed</u>. I really <u>loved</u> <u>the soup</u>. A good <u>meal</u> is <u>something I always enjoy</u>. I look forward to <u>having you over, too</u>.

Thank you for <u>a great dinner</u>.

Option 2: Want an even easier note to write?

The note that follows is super easy!

Instant Thank-You
Note for Gifts

Thank you for the <u>describing word</u>   <u>name the gift.</u>
(world-class/colorful/   *(tennis racquet/book/*
newly released/delicious/   *flowers/vase/phone/*
sumptuous/invigorating/   *pouch/shirt)*
elegant/tailored)

The thought and the gift are valued. Your gift was especially nice

because <u>see descriptive words for ideas, page 22.</u>
(it will improve my game/it's useful/it was timely/
it will help me decorate my den)

I appreciate you and the nice gift.

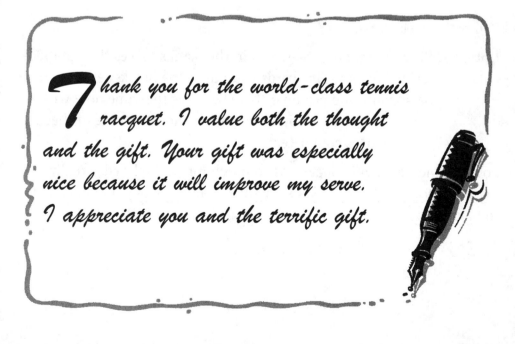

Thank you for the world-class tennis racquet. I value both the thought and the gift. Your gift was especially nice because it will improve my serve. I appreciate you and the terrific gift.

Instant Thank-You
Note for Events
(Dinners/Fundraisers/Parties/
Meetings/Social Occasions)

Thank you for including me in the <u>describing word, page 22</u>

<u>name the event</u>. I value the <u>day/evening/time/etc.</u>.
(birthday party/dinner/
annual meeting/fundraiser)

The event was especially good because <u>see descriptive words, page 22.</u>
(I got to see my neighbors/you're a
great cook/it helped me to get to know
my co-workers better/the food was
great/it was such a fun time/it was so
well planned)

I appreciate your inviting me.

Thank you for including me in the beautifully planned Annual Meeting. I value the time. The event was especially good because it helped me get to know my co-workers. I appreciate your inviting me.

Thank-You Letter for an Event (Dinners, Meetings, Fundraisers)

Your invitation to join you for <u>name of event</u> meant a great deal to me. From the _____ to the _____, your message came through clearly: <u>theme/message</u>.

Thank you for including me in this memorable <u>event</u>.
(day/meeting)

Your invitation to join you for your annual stockholder's meeting meant a great deal to me. From the globes on each table to the international speakers, your message came through clearly: Southern Company truly is a global company now.

Thank you for including me in this momentous event.

Thank You for Thoughtfulness

Your thoughtfulness in <u>offering to drive me to Nancy's wedding</u> is greatly
(inviting my son/inviting the new student to your party)

appreciated. Thank you for thinking of <u>me</u> in such a nice way. Meeting
(us/him)

nice folks like you along the way adds a great deal to our lives.

Again, thank you for being so thoughtful.

Want More Ideas?

- Tell how the gift/event made you feel. Try using some of the words on the following page.
- What will the gift help you do? See page 35.
- Try to use more words from pages 22–24.

Positive Feeling Words—Tell How the Gift Made You Feel

acknowledged	esteemed	pampered
active	excited	peaceful
adamant	fantastic	pleased
aggressive	fine	positive
alert	fortunate	potent
alive	friendly	powerful
amused	glad	proud
appreciated	good	quick
bold	great	reassured
brave	happy	recognized
calm	heady	relaxed
capable	healthy	relieved
celebrated	honored	rewarded
cheerful	hopeful	satisfied
camaraderie	intense	secure
confident	invigorated	solid
content	justify	super
delighted	loud	thankful
determined	loving	thrilled
ecstatic	mellow	tough
elated	motherly	turned on
energetic	on an exciting threshold	up
	on top of the world	warm
	open	well dressed

Verb List
What Will the Gift Help You Do?

accelerate	give	return
add	guide	ride
adorn	help	save
aid	hold	send
allow	include	serve
answer	inform	share
begin	interact	sharpen
bring	invite	shorten
buy	join	shut
change	lead	signify
communicate	let	sort
complete	light	spread
compliment	locate	stake
conquer	look	start
cook	make	stock
coordinate	mark	store
correct	meet	suggest
develop	mend	supply
discover	offer	support
distribute	open	swim
do	organize	switch
elevate	participate	take
erase	pay	talk
expand	permit	tear
expedite	play	touch
extend	position	travel
find	present	try
finish	produce	underscore
fit	provide	use
fix	put	watch
flourish	raise	work
get	record	write
grow	relate	zip

NOTES FOR ALL OCCASIONS

On the following pages, you will find some of the most useful samples of notes to send to friends, neighbors, co-workers, and acquaintances. You will use these basic forms many times over the years, but you will make each note unique and meaningful to the receiver. How? Use your own words to fill in the blanks and create a very personal note.

In other words, if you are writing to ask a favor, you will need to fill in one blank stating the favor and another blank that describes what needs to be done. How much easier could writing be?

Get Well

Here's hoping that this note finds you feeling somewhat better. I was sorry to hear that you have a cold.
(broke your leg/
contracted measles/
had surgery)

Take care of yourself and know that I'm thinking of you.
(saying prayers for
your recovery)

For a longer letter:

I especially hope you recover quickly. You may find it helpful to read the article in this month's *Reader's Digest* on vitamin C.
(drink lots of fluids/take it easier than usual/keep your feet elevated)

Let's hope you're on the mend soon.

Cheer Up

Just thought you might need a friendly word about now. When you consider all the wonderful things you've done and the special person
(your contributions/your overall season)   (the many good choices you've made/your many options)

you are, you might be encouraged that things will improve.

I'm looking forward to hearing that you're feeling better.
(rejuvenated/your usual joy/at peace/ encouraged)

Appreciation

I very much appreciated your writing that letter of recommendation.
(sending me the newspaper clipping/sharing your bushel of apples with me/recommending me for promotion/driving carpool for me Tuesday)

Because you took the time to help me, I want to take a moment to let you know how much it meant to me. In fact, I appreciate many things about you.
(your work/ your company/ your services)

For a longer letter:

You really made me feel special. Your thoughtfulness did not go unnoticed.
(acknowledged/   (offer/help)
pampered, or some other positive feeling word from page 34)

Expressing Friendship—New Friend

This is a note to let you know how much I enjoy <u>the time we spend together.</u>
(carpooling together/working with you/serving on the task force with you)

It isn't often that I run across someone who <u>shares such similar interests.</u>
(enjoys the out of doors as I do/works at such a similar pace/sees political issues so similarly/enjoys these projects too/is as artistic as you are)

So often our observations about nice people go unsaid. I don't want to make that mistake. Thank you for enriching my life with your companionship.

Expressing Friendship—Old Friend

When someone is a real friend, like you, we're tempted to feel so comfortable that we never say some things we probably should. Your friendship means a great deal to me. I don't want to be guilty of taking that for granted. That's why I am writing to you today.

One thing I especially value about you is <u>that we can spend time alone with no agenda and still have a good time.</u>
(your sense of humor/your easygoing approach to life/your loyalty)

It is my goal to be just as good a friend to you as you are to me.

Comfort

At a time like this, I can offer little except my sincere wish for your comfort. Please know that you are in my <u>thoughts</u>. You certainly are
(prayers)
facing a difficult time.

If there is anything I can do in the coming weeks, please call on me.

I hope you count me among those who want to be supportive of you during this time of sadness.

Condolences—Family Member

You are in my <u>thoughts</u> at this time. Please accept my <u>condolences on</u> the
(prayers)   *(sympathy for)*
loss of your <u>mother</u>.
(father/aunt)

OPTION 1: If in any way I can offer my help or comfort, please do not hesitate to call.

OPTION 2: Whenever I think of your <u>mother</u>, I will always remember
(father)

her <u>great brownies</u>.
(sense of humor)

You are a valued <u>friend</u>, and I hope you know that you are
(neighbor/co-worker)

cared about and supported in this difficult time.

 NOTE: *You may choose both options. Feel free to elaborate. You are not limited to a single sentence as shown in the example.*

Condolences—Friend

I know you must be feeling a tremendous sense of loss right now.

The death of a friend is always difficult, and <u>Ella</u> was an especially
(deceased's name)

wonderful person.

My <u>sympathy</u> goes out to you now in your time of grief. If I can be
(condolences/heart)

there for you in any way, please just let me know.

CHAPTER

4

TOUCHY SITUATIONS

- How do I create a positive tone if the situation is negative?

- How do I make an apology sound sincere?

- How do I say "no" but still convey my regard for the reader?

TIPS: HOW TO WRITE A SINCERE, EFFECTIVE APOLOGY

An effective apology letter addresses *two* key issues:

- The incident or mistake that requires the apology

- The reader's feelings

By far the most important issue is the reader's feelings. Believe it or not, to many people the incident or problem is far less important than how it made them feel. For example, if you spill wine on your friend's carpet, the spot is a problem that must be taken care of—by you, of course. Far more important to your friend may be how she or he felt about the *way* the incident happened. Whether your friend's feelings or perceptions are valid really doesn't matter. You must address the real or imagined feelings in your letter. For example, let's take the incident of the spilled wine. Did your friend perhaps feel one of the following emotions?

- Concerned because her carpet was new

- Stressed because she had already had a bad day

- Disappointed because she thought your act was careless

- Anxious because she was just house-sitting the apartment

When you address the reader's feelings, you show empathy. When you show empathy, you have a caring, highly effective letter of apology. Letters of apology can sound perfunctory and cold if not handled sensitively. Putting in a feeling word or empathy statement can make your apology sound sincere and heartfelt.

Try to imagine how the other person felt when the incident or problem occurred. Did she feel anxious? Disappointed? Hurt? Rushed? Outraged? For a list of "Feeling Words" to draw from, see page 45. Of course, there are many more feelings than are listed. If the feeling words listed don't describe your reader's feeling, use the list to jog your imagination.

TIPS: HOW TO WRITE AN EMPATHY STATEMENT

Somewhere the letter should contain an empathy statement. Empathy statements make good use of the feeling words. Empathy statements do just what they say: they say to your reader, "I can understand how you feel." Below you will find some examples of empathy statements. Use these in your next apology letter or make up your own ways to express empathy.

- You must have felt embarrassed when the video monitor for your presentation didn't arrive.

- I can see why you might feel hurt because I didn't make it to your open house.

- Because I didn't arrive on time, you probably felt let down.

- You must have felt surprised when I didn't show up on time to pick up the children.

- Looking at the situation from your side, I see that <u>my sending you the bill</u> must have made you feel <u>uneasy</u>.

- It can feel <u>frightening</u> when <u>you go to the office at night to meet someone who doesn't show</u>.

- I can see how you might have felt that <u>I was disrespectful when I allowed my children to use markers near your sofa</u>.

Personalizing Your Empathy Statement

In each of the empathy statements above, you find that you must fill in two blanks. Two issues are addressed in every empathy statement:

- The incident

- The reader's feelings

When you want to tailor these empathy statements so that you can write your own apology, simply change what is in the blanks. In one blank, simply and briefly describe the problem or incident. For the other blank, choose a feeling word from page 45. What you'll have is a unique and very personal apology. Your reader will appreciate the sensitivity.

Empathy Words

afraid	frail	resentful
aggravated	frightened	run-down
amazed	frustrated	rushed
angry	furious	shaky
annoyed	gloomy	shy
anxious	glum	sick
apathetic	guilty	skeptical
ashamed	hate	slighted
awed	helpless	sore
awful	hopeless	sorry
awkward	horrible	stuck
bad	horrified	stunned
baffled	hurt	surprised
betrayed	ill	taken off guard
blue	inadequate	tense
bored	infuriated	terrible
bothered	insecure	terrified
challenged	intimidated	timid
confused	irritated	tired
crushed	jumpy	trapped
dazed	justified	troubled
defenseless	lifeless	turned off
depressed	lonely	unbelieving
disappointed	lost	uncertain
discouraged	low	uncomfortable
disgusted	mad	uneasy
disorganized	mean	unhappy
displaced	miserable	unloved
disrespected	nervous	unsupported
dissatisfied	obligated	unsure
distracted	outraged	upset
disturbed	overwhelmed	useless
doubtful	painful	vulnerable
down	perplexed	weak
embarrassed	powerless	wistful
enraged	pushed	weary
exhausted	puzzled	wilted
fearful	quiet	worn out
fragile	rage	worried

All-Purpose Apology Letter

Please accept my sincere apology. You must have felt <u>concerned</u> when
(perplexed/hurt/
upset/Empathy Word,
page 45)

<u>I failed to notify you of the deadline for signing up for the golf tournament.</u>
(I returned your VCR so late)

I regret any inconvenience it may have caused you.

<u>For a longer letter:</u>

I hope you will allow me to <u>pay your late fee</u>. I value <u>your friendship</u>
(other compensation)   *(our relationship/your*
business/your being
such a good neighbor)

and wish this had never occurred.

STANDARD APOLOGY LETTERS

Business Apology

You deserve an apology for <u>the delay in your order</u>. You must have felt
                                 (the damage to your shipment/
                                 the mix up in your delivery)

<u>frustrated</u> when <u>it didn't arrive</u>. Please accept my assurance that we are
(Empathy Word,   *(describe incident)*
page 45)

taking steps to ensure this does not happen again to a valued <u>customer</u>
                                                 (employee/vendor/
                                                 guest/visitor/tenant/
                                                 resident)

like you. I am sorry for all the inconvenience.

For a longer letter:

Also, we would like to offer <u>to pay the shipping charges</u>. Please let me
                                      (to discount your next order/
                                      to have our crew set up the
                                        equipment for you)

know if this would be acceptable to you.

Damage to Home/Property

You can imagine how sorry I am that I backed my car into your storage

(that my pen leaked on your leather topped

desk/about my diskette that transmitted the

computer virus/that my children flooded your

carpeted bathroom)

building. Please accept my apology for this regrettable incident. You

(accident, damage)

must have felt troubled when you saw the hole in the corner wall.

(Empathy Word,   *(found the damage/came home)*

page 45/appalled/

disappointed)

I am sorry.

For a longer letter:

Please allow me to have my favorite carpenter fix the damage. I regret

(suggest compensation)

any inconvenience that this has caused you.

....

NOTE: *Use a colon after the greeting if this is a business acquaintance. Use a comma if the reader is a personal acquaintance or friend. You can learn more about the correct formats for personal letters in Chapter Thirteen.*

Thoughtlessness

It's difficult to tell you just how much I regret what happened. You
must have felt <u>embarrassed</u> when <u>I failed to show up at the restaurant</u>
             (Empathy Word,   *(state problem)*
             page 45)
<u>on Saturday</u>. It's my hope that you know that I would never intentionally
disappoint you.

For a longer letter:

Although it is no excuse, I want you to know that <u>I had written down</u>
                                              (had mistakenly believed
                                              the event was cancelled/
                                              was being held at gun-
                                              point in a bank robbery)

<u>the date incorrectly</u>. Once again, I am sorry for my mistake.

Forgetfulness

My sincere apology is all I can offer for forgetting <u>to leave your apartment</u>
                                              (our appointment/
                                              your birthday)

<u>key under the mat</u>. You must have felt <u>frustrated</u> because <u>I left you with</u>
                                          (disappointed/angry)

<u>no way to enter your apartment after your long trip</u>.
(I wasted so much of your valuable time/it should have been a special time)

For a longer letter:

Please allow me to <u>pay for the locksmith</u>. My actions may not prove it,
                          (reschedule/take you out)

but I do value your <u>time</u>. Again, I am sorry and hope you will forgive
                       (friendship/business/feelings)

this mistake on my part.

Misunderstanding—
Writer Is at Fault

I regret more than you know our recent misunderstanding. Please

forgive me for <u>criticizing your resume</u>. You must have felt <u>disappointed</u>
(arguing with you about your choice of schools/   *(Empathy Word,*
being disagreeable/speaking out of turn/offering   *page 45/*
my unsolicited and invalid opinion)   *annoyed/hurt)*

that I <u>overlooked your job experience</u>. You are a valued <u>friend</u>. Please
(interrupted you/spoke sharply/didn't   *(business associate/*
give you the credit due you)   *neighbor)*

accept my sincere apology.

Misunderstanding—
Reader Is at Fault

I sincerely regret our recent misunderstanding. You are a valued <u>friend</u>.
(business associate/
team member)

I hope we can put this behind us soon.

For my part, I feel I could have <u>reacted differently</u>.
(waited until a better
time to talk to you)

<u>For a longer letter:</u>

Maybe you can understand that <u>at first I felt let down</u>.
(I felt my work had been criticized/
I was hurt by the suddenness of your
leaving/I was taken off guard)

At your earliest convenience, let's <u>talk about this again</u>.
(try the meeting again/try to resume
our project, friendship, workouts)

Again, it's my hope we can work this out together.

LETTERS DEALING WITH OTHER TOUCHY SITUATIONS

Uninviting Guests

This is without a doubt an embarrassing letter to write. We need

to cancel <u>our dinner plans for February 9th</u> because
(our trip to our mountain cabin)

<u>my company is requiring that I attend a seminar that week.</u>
(my daughter had made plans prior to ours)

You know how much we value <u>spending time with you</u>. Only
(your business/your friendship)

a situation like this could force me to cancel.

<u>For a longer letter</u>:

May we reschedule for <u>May 5th</u>? Thank you for being understanding
(Date/Time)

about this. I look forward to seeing you then, if that works for you.

Declining Invitations

I regret that I won't be able to join you for your <u>anniversary celebration</u>
(Event)

on <u>May 2nd</u>. You <u>party</u> sounds <u>wonderful</u>, but <u>I will be out of town</u>.
(Date)   *(Event)*   *(fun/stimulating/*   *(we previously had*
Word List,   *made plans)*
page 22)*

Thank you for including me. Your event will be a great success, I'm sure.

Changing Plans

It looks as though we need to make a change. It seems that
<u>the school needs you to sponsor the Beta Club after all</u>.
*(we can't refund your deposit/you are not certified
to lifeguard at the community pool/the opening
in Human Resources requires an advanced degree)*

<u>You were looking forward to freeing up some afterschool time</u>,
*(You had hoped to interview for the position/
You wished to lifeguard for us as your summer job/
You had counted on receiving the money)*

I'm sure. Please accept my apology for any inconvenience that this
may cause you.

<u>For a longer letter:</u>

Would it work for you if we <u>changed the meeting time?</u>
(talked to you again after you've taken the Red
Cross course/did our transactions online next time)

Thank you for your <u>cooperation</u>.
(flexibility/time)

Pointing Out Someone's Mistake

It was a pleasure to talk with you <u>at the family reunion last week</u>. I
(on the phone yesterday)

particularly enjoyed <u>your reminiscences about Jerry's childhood</u>.
(state one pleasant uncontroversial thing)

Because I thought you would want to know, I am writing to tell you

<u>that the woman with Jerry was not his wife; she is a friend</u>.
(state incorrect information and follow with correction)

I knew that you would want to know the correct information. Since

we are <u>relatives</u>, I felt you would prefer to hear it from me.
(friends/co-workers)

I hope you would do the same for me.

....

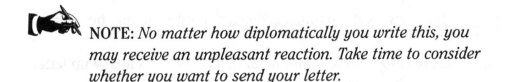 NOTE: *No matter how diplomatically you write this, you may receive an unpleasant reaction. Take time to consider whether you want to send your letter.*

Returning Gifts

You were so kind to give me the <u>lovely salad bowl</u>. It meant so much to
(stylish bracelet)

me that you remembered me so thoughtfully.

Unfortunately, I must return your special gift. <u>John and I have broken</u>

<u>our engagement and are returning all gifts</u>.
(The bracelet is much too expensive for me to accept)

Thank you for your understanding. I do appreciate your thought and
effort in giving me such a nice gift.

Did My Gift Arrive?
Checking Up

<u>Weddings</u> always create so much activity. You must be very busy, but I
(Graduations/Birthdays)

hope you are enjoying every minute of it. This is just a follow-up letter

to the gift I sent. I wanted to make sure it was delivered by <u>UPS</u> as I
(Federal Express/
Macy's)

had arranged.

Service and delivery problems happen. I just wanted to make sure you
have the gift and that it arrived intact.

Please call anytime to let me know.

Have a wonderful <u>wedding</u>.
(39th year/graduation)

Asking a Favor

I hope this letter finds you well and <u>excited about summer vacation</u>.
(enjoying your new job)

You and I should get together soon to catch up on news.

I am writing today to ask a favor. You have always been such a good

<u>friend</u> that I feel I can ask you to <u>loan me your car for the weekend of</u>
(neighbor/co-worker)   *(specific favor)*

<u>July 18–20, 2000</u>.

<u>I will be driving my son to college and don't have a car now that we've</u>

<u>moved to the city</u>.
(purpose or reason for favor)

As always, I hope you will be candid and comfortable about telling me

how you feel about this. You remain a valued <u>person in my life</u>.
(co-worker/relative)

NOTE: *Sometimes you can begin a letter like this with a quote. Example: "'Ask a busy person if you want something done' is the conventional wisdom."*

CONGRATULATIONS

Celebrating Achievements and Milestones

•

How to Write a Note of Congratulations

•

Standard Letters of Congratulations

- How do I add a personal twist and a real tone of celebration?

- How do I make this event special for the reader?

- How do I write a note that doesn't sound perfunctory or obligatory?

- How do I acknowledge a unique accomplishment or event?

CELEBRATING ACHIEVEMENTS AND MILESTONES

One of the happiest reasons to write a note is to congratulate another person on an accomplishment or key event in his or her life. From landing that dream job to joyously announcing the birth of a first child, our friends and acquaintances have many milestones in their lives. One of the most meaningful and memorable things you can ever do for them is to recognize each milestone with a unique note acknowledging just how special this event is. If you write a note of congratulations well, it may find its way into someone's special file of keepsakes or memorabilia. In some cases, your note may be the only documentation of a very special time in a reader's life. How's that for motivation for writing notes of congratulations?

HOW TO WRITE A NOTE OF CONGRATULATIONS

All congratulatory notes have three elements in common:

1. The event must be stated clearly and briefly. Spell it out: "the birth of your daughter" or "the promotion to Senior Engineer II."

2. Your admiration, enthusiasm, joy, or some other positive emotion must be stated: "I was delighted to hear that you've become parents" or "As a witness to all your years of effort, I share in your joy in this accomplishment" or "From the sidelines, I have watched you prepare yourself for a promotion like this, and I'm happy that you achieved your goal."

3. A great closing for a congratulatory note is an exhortation. An exhortation focuses the reader on the future. Here are some sample exhortations that could end notes of congratulations:

   - May this be just the first step up the corporate ladder for you.

   - Here's hoping you enjoy your beautiful new home for years to come.

   - My prayers are with you for a long and happy life together.

If you follow the steps above, you will send out notes of congratulation that make your reader feel acknowledged in a special way.

STANDARD LETTERS OF CONGRATULATIONS

Congratulations—Promotion

Your much-deserved promotion gives me an excuse to tell you how pleased I am at your success. <u>Appointing you to the office</u> of
(position)

<u>senior vice president</u> shows that others acknowledge your <u>ability</u>.
(controller/supervisor)   *(hard work/*
effort to enhance
your education)

Congratulations on this exciting promotion. May this be just one of many upward moves in a fulfilling career.

Congratulations—New Job

The news about your <u>exciting</u> new job is a reason to celebrate.
(visible/fascinating/
demanding/exotic/
philanthropic)

Congratulations on being selected from what I'm sure was a competitive field. May this job bring you interesting days, many rewards, and a bright future.

NOTE: *The "Promotion" letter above can also be adapted for a new job.*

Congratulations—Birth/Adoption

Your new baby <u>girl</u> and all the joy <u>she</u> will bring you has <u>us</u> celebrating.
     (boy)   *(he)*   *(me)*

Congratulations on such a <u>blessed</u> event. Our <u>thoughts</u> will be with you
                                    (momentous/   *(prayers)*
                                    happy)

as you nurture this child at the beginning of <u>her</u> life and in the future.
                                                         (his)

<u>We</u> <u>are</u> wishing both you and this fortunate child a lifetime of love and
(I) *(am)*

<u>blessing</u>.
(success/good fortune)

Congratulations—New Home

Congratulations on your new home. You must be especially pleased

because <u>your new neighborhood is one of the best in our city</u>. A move
        (the home is new and has so many modern features/homes
        in the historic district are rare finds/you've planned this for
        so long/this house has a pool, extra bedroom, etc.)

like this is another milestone for you. May this house bring you many

years of joy and contentment.

Congratulations—Achievement

You have set yourself apart by <u>being selected as a delegate to the</u> <u>Democratic National Convention.</u>
(joining Mensa/being named Employee of the Year)

Congratulations on this outstanding achievement. You certainly deserve it. May this accomplishment be only one of many paving the road to a bright future for you.

Congratulations—Marriage

Congratulations on your <u>upcoming</u> marriage. Two people
(recent)

<u>with so much in common</u> should be together. Best wishes for a
(who are so in love/who are so nice)

wonderful and fulfilling life together.

 NOTE: *If you are writing the note prior to the marriage, you should be aware of an old tradition. Traditionalists say that the writer should write "Congratulations" to the groom and "Best wishes" to the bride. If you are writing to someone who might follow these conventions, you may wish to adapt your language to this tradition. The choice is yours.*

Congratulations—Award

Your success in winning the <u>Good Neighbor Award</u> for your
  (name award)

<u>Cobb leadership Initiative Project</u> is much deserved.
(service/work on behalf of homeless animals)

I want to convey my respect and admiration for you.

Congratulations, <u>Betty</u>. I am so pleased that your <u>dedication</u> has been
  (name)   *(academic excellence/*
                                                         talents)

acknowledged in this memorable way.

Congratulations—Retirement

Congratulations on your <u>upcoming</u> retirement. You can look back with
  (recent)

a real sense of accomplishment on a job well done. I wish you well as

you enjoy the next chapter of your life. You certainly deserve the best

wishes and admiration of all who <u>know you</u>.
                              (worked with you/love you)

Keep me posted on <u>how your golf game improves</u>. I hope that's just one
  (how your new catering business goes/all your
  volunteer work you now have time for)

of the many joys of your retirement.

CHAPTER

6

SOCIAL OCCASIONS

Tips: Managing Your Social Life

•

Invitations That People Respond To

•

Standard Invitations

•

Announcements

- How do I make sure my invitations help my guests arrive on the right day, at the right time, and at the right place? How can I prevent someone from making an embarrassing mistake?

- How do I write announcements that convey my sincere warmth and happiness, but still give the reader the necessary details?

- How can I contribute to the celebratory nature of an event by the way I announce, write, or respond in my letters?

TIPS: MANAGING YOUR SOCIAL LIFE

We could learn a lot about managing our personal lives from business. Many of us are so busy that we feel we can be careless about the details of our social correspondence. We often manage our business appointments well, but our personal lives are haphazard. If we are not as careful about a personal letter as we are about a business letter, however, the results could be embarrassing or worse.

This applies especially to invitations. If we truly want our personal invitations to be read accurately and responded to promptly, we need to take some TIPS from business. Business letters make sure that the readers get the facts straight and answer as quickly as possible. Isn't this what we want when we send out invitations for a social event?

INVITATIONS THAT PEOPLE RESPOND TO

To cut down on confusion and slow responses, businesses use these techniques that we should adopt for our personal invitations:

1. Put all pertinent information in bulleted lists:

   - Time

   - Date

   - Location

2. At the beginning of the invitation, try to put what's in it for the invitee. If you are inviting people to a charity event, you could begin like this:

   "How can you have a day of fun, save on your taxes, and help some wonderful but needy children at the same time? Join us for the Walnut Hill Annual Bass Fishing Tournament."

3. Make clear how you want people to respond. For RSVPs, give telephone numbers that actually answer or else provide a voice mailbox. If you choose voice mail, be sure to ask your invitees to leave a message. If not, some very polite people will keep trying until they can respond to you personally. If you include an RSVP, make it visible and compelling. Don't let it get lost in a paragraph. Your invitations can still be warm and personal even if you take the steps above. These TIPS borrowed from business can assure that people get to your event on the right day at the right time.

All-Purpose Invitation

You are invited to attend an event that will surely be a lot of fun.
*(help needy children
in our community/be
welcomed by everyone
who will attend/be an
occasion to remember/
be memorable/be a
surprise to my husband,
Jack/bring together many
wonderful friends)*

I am writing to invite you to a 1960s theme party. The plans are under-
*(Jack's birthday party/
a fundraiser for UNICEF)*

way, and this is shaping up to be a great night for all who can attend.
*(afternoon/
event)*

I hope you can be there to join us in this celebration. The details follow:

- Date: Saturday, January 21, 2000
- Time: 3:00 – 5:00 P.M.
- Place: Willows Pavilion

    Chastain Park
- RSVP: Jane Ayre (555) 666-7777 by January 15.

    Please leave a voice mail message.

Have no doubt that your being there is important to us. I'm looking
forward to hearing whether you will be part of this celebration.
(hoe-down/event)

STANDARD INVITATIONS

Milestone Birthday Invitation

<u>Josh Evans</u> has reached a milestone: He's turning <u>40</u>. We want you to
(name of honoree)   *(60/30)*

join us to celebrate it. For <u>Josh's 40th</u> birthday, we are planning to
                                        (name (60th/30th)
                                        of honoree)

honor him with a <u>fish fry</u>. The party won't be complete without you,
                        (cocktail party/party at home/cookout)

so please plan to join us. These are the details:

- DATE: Saturday, July 21, 2000
- TIME: 1:00 – 3:00 P.M.
- PLACE: Our House

  3237 Matador Lane
- RSVP: Emily Bronx (555) 666-7777 by July 14.

  Please leave a message.

Help us usher in a great new decade for <u>Josh</u>. I look forward to hearing
                                            (name of honoree)

from you soon.

Parties/Dinners—Version One

We are putting together a <u>dinner</u> so that we can spend time with some
(cocktail party)

special people like you. The <u>evening</u> will not be complete without your
(afternoon)

presence. Here are the details:

- DATE: Saturday, April 21, 2000
- TIME: 7:00 P.M.
- PLACE: 111 Mockingbird Lane
- RSVP: Scout Radley (555) 666-7777 by April 14.

  Please leave a voice mail message.

This should be a <u>warm</u> and <u>harmonious</u> gathering. I hope to hear from
(casual/   (see Word List,
friendly)   page 22)

you soon, saying you will join us.

Parties/Dinners—Version Two

Please join us for an evening that we hope will be as special for you as it will be for us. You are invited to join us for a dinner party to reunite some old friends and get better acquainted with some new ones. We hope you can be with us as our very special guest. The particulars are as follows:

- DATE: Saturday, April 21, 2000
- TIME: 7:00 P.M.
- PLACE: 111 Mockingbird Lane
- RSVP: Scout Radley (555) 666-7777 by April 14.

        Please leave a voice mail message.

We look forward to the pleasure of your company.

Reunion

A reunion is a great way to get to see people we miss, like you. Please say you will join us for the Hilliard Family Reunion. Many dear relatives
(Smith High School's Reunion of   (old friends)
the Class of '68)

will be attending this ambitious event. Here are the details:
(significant)

- DATE: Saturday, June 18, 2000
- TIME: 6:00 P.M.
- PLACE: Marriott Hotel

    2300 Canton Road

    Smyrna, GA (map enclosed)
- RSVP: Janine Edgars Hill (555) 666-7777 by June 10.

    Please leave a message.

This reunion will not be complete without your presence. We hope to hear from you soon.

Anniversary Celebrations

A wonderful event to celebrate is coming up and you are invited.

<u>John and Marilyn Foster have been married for 25 years!</u> Please join
(change names and years)

us for a festive anniversary <u>dinner</u> to honor this memorable milestone
(party/luncheon)

in their lives.

- DATE: Saturday, February 22, 2000
- TIME: 6:00 P.M.
- PLACE: Sheraton Hotel

            1285 and Piedmont Road
- RSVP: Lisa Bova (555) 666-7777 by February 15.

            Please leave a message on voice mail.

We hope you will be with us for this <u>evening</u> of fun and a little nostalgia.
(afternoon/day)

Invitation to House Guest

You are one person I just don't seem to see enough of, it seems.

Why don't you join us as our house guest for <u>a weekend</u>? We could
*(a week at our
beach house)*

<u>get caught up</u> and <u>go to the Matisse Exhibit at the High Museum.</u>
(stay up late   (attend the Smith's 40th Anniversary party together/
talking/play   have coffee together every morning)
tennis/fish/shop)

I know that you are busy and it will take some arranging, but please

say you'll be our guest. <u>The weekend that I am suggesting is</u>
(Why don't you come in early March?)

<u>June 21–23.</u>

Are you up for it? Please give me a call soon when you have had a

chance to check your calendar.

All-Occasion—Happy "Anything" Day

Happy Mother's Day! On this special day, I am sending my heartfelt
(name of event being celebrated)

wishes for your happiness and health. You deserve to have a really

great day for all the happiness you have brought others.
(all the lives you have touched/all the years you've
given as a mother/those wonderful qualities that
make you who you are)

On this Mother's Day, I hope you will find time to do something you
(celebration)

enjoy, like read a novel. Your day will be as relaxing as you like, I trust.
(visit with Lois)   (active)

To celebrate, I'm sending you tickets to the Braves game. As for me,
(this letter full of my love and best wishes)

I'll be spending the day working in my garden, a labor of love.
(having lunch with my son)

Again, enjoy this special day and know that I am thinking of you

with love.
(fondness)

RSVP

I frequently hear from hostesses the lament that people have become lax about responding to invitations with an RSVP. ("RSVP" may be capitalized or lowercase.) A written invitation with an RSVP *requires* a written response. RSVP stands for repondez s'il vous plait. This simply means, "Please reply." That's exactly what a host needs guests to do. A good host must make plans for food, seating, and service. Honoring an RSVP on a note is a must.

A very formal invitation requires that you basically repeat all the particulars of the invitation in the order that they appeared in the invitation. The following invitation works well for most formal and informal invitations.

I am writing to respond to your <u>kind</u> invitation to <u>attend the fortieth</u>
                                    (fun/thoughtful)   *(state what invitation is for)*

<u>birthday party you are giving for Ron</u>. You can count on <u>Sam and me</u>
                                                                (state all attendees)

to be <u>at your home on May 9th</u> at <u>7:00</u> P.M.
    (It's helpful to restate dates, time, locations,
    but not necessary)

We are very much looking forward to it.

ANNOUNCEMENTS

Birth Announcement

A wonderful baby boy has entered our lives. <u>Jared</u> and I are <u>ecstatic</u> to
(spouse's name) (happy/pleased)

announce the birth of little <u>Harrison Drew Bentley</u>. <u>His</u> vital statistics
(newborn's name) (Her)

are as follows:

- Born at <u>7:35 P.M. on Monday, June 25, 2000</u>

- Weighed in at <u>7 pounds 2 ounces</u>

- <u>21" long, blue eyes, no hair</u>

Thank you for sharing in our joy at this much-anticipated event.

 NOTE: *Add your comments about the baby's features or cute things he does or your own responses to this event. Personal comments aren't trivial; they add zest to these and other types of letters.*

Engagement

An exciting change has taken place in my life, and I want to share it with you.

I recently became engaged to <u>Claudia Owens</u>, and we plan to marry
(fiancée/fiancé)

<u>after I finish my residency.</u>
(soon/next year/in June)

<u>Claudia</u> and I met <u>here in Evansville</u> and have dated <u>ever since.</u> She is a
(fiancée/fiancé)   *(at karate lessons/*   *(for over a year)*
          on the job/at church)

<u>partner with Phillips & Roth, Attorneys at Law</u> and enjoys
(teacher/musician)

<u>many of the things I do, like fly fishing.</u> We hope you share in our joy.
(opera and Irish dancing/the same
oldies music/tennis and golf)

We look forward to sharing, as a couple, a wonderful future that includes <u>friends</u> like you.
(relatives)

Wedding Announcement

Ariadna and I plan to marry and want you to attend our small, but special, wedding. You are a valuable part of our lives and we hope you can attend this event that holds so much significance for us. Our plans are as follows:

- Ceremony and reception at the home of

  Mr. and Mrs. James Jenks

  2222 Ellwood Drive

  Olympia, GA
- DATE: Saturday, November 30, 1999
- TIME: 6:00 P.M.
- RSVP: Ariadna Jenks at (555) 666-7777 by November 23.

  Please leave a voice mail message.

Both of us are hoping very much that you will join us for this joyous occasion.

 NOTE: *A formal wedding announcement will be engraved by your stationer. He/She will have formats for a formal announcement. This is the less formal style, recommended for a letter.*

Marriage Announcement

<u>Arnold</u> and I are so pleased to share some good news with you. We were
(spouse's name)

married last week in <u>Carmel, California</u>, and couldn't wait to let you
(at a small civil service/in my parents' home)

know.

As you know, <u>Arnold</u> and I <u>share many lifelong interests, such as the</u>
        (spouse's   (have dated for several years/have looked forward
          name)   to this day for a long time)

<u>theater and travel</u>.

Thank you for participating in our joy at this wonderful event in our

lives.

....

 NOTE: *Include any pertinent details such as where you
will live and if other changes will follow (name changes,
adoptions).*

Death

With great sorrow, we are writing to let you know of the death of

<u>my mother, Janet Foster</u>. She died <u>of a stroke</u> last week
(name of person)   (cause of death)

<u>in Premier Hospital in Acworth, Georgia</u>.
(at home/after a long illness)

Please join us in remembering <u>her warm laughter and her ability to see</u>
                                             (her wonderful work for the American Diabetes
                                             Association/her hospitality and her quick wit)
<u>the good in everyone</u>.

Thank you for being part of <u>our lives</u> and for your friendship.
                                  (her life)

....

NOTE: *If you think the reader will send flowers and you prefer a charitable donation, write something like the following to express your preference.*

Your thoughts and prayers are valuable to us. If you are considering sending flowers, you might consider a donation to my mother's favorite charity, the <u>United Way</u>.
                    (American Diabetes Association/
                    Habitat for Humanity)

CHAPTER

7

LIFE
CHANGES

Expressing Change in Positive Terms

•

Standard Letters Relating to Life Changes

- How can I convey the particulars of my new life-style, schedule, location, or other change in a clear way so my friends can communicate with me?

- How do I communicate my life change as an opportunity to emerge triumphant?

- How can I communicate about death and illness sensitively yet honestly?

EXPRESSING CHANGE IN POSITIVE TERMS

Change can be a welcome or unwelcome event in one's life. Even the most positive change can evoke a flurry of emotions from both the writer and the reader. In almost every case, the best policy is to keep letters that chronicle change in our lives as positive and upbeat as possible.

Some examples of life changes and how our letters announcing those life changes can stir up emotions are listed below:

You announce with excitement your long-awaited retirement. You view it as a reward for years of hard work. You write to your friend, whom you haven't seen in several years. Your friend lost a job and was forced to take early retirement a few years ago. Due to different circumstances, your friend views retirement as a negative event. Your friend needs to hear the news of your retirement in a positive way.

You move to a different state as a result of a job transfer. Don't portray yourself as a victim of corporate America. Instead, create a picture of yourself as a versatile and talented employee whose career is on the move. Our mobile, ever-changing population creates a lot of opportunities for letters dealing with life changes. Friends and relatives will welcome your letters if you focus on the excitement of new possibilities. Even if this change is the result of a sad event, like a divorce, you will win more support if you share your constructive plans for a new future rather than your bitter observations about your unfortunate situation. One friend told me, "Any time I ever threw myself a pity party, no one showed up."

Remember, too, that regrets and recriminations that may sound acceptable in a conversation may seem much harsher when put in writing. Don't forget, either, that letters live on. Letters record your feelings and attitudes, and they may change as the years go by. You may wish that you had never put your negative thoughts in writing.

Here are a few positives you can focus on in your next letter announcing a change in your life:

- What are your plans?
    - ☞ Will you travel?
    - ☞ Where will you live?
    - ☞ Will your children change schools?
    - ☞ Does it affect your job or volunteer responsibilities?
- Will the change mean a move closer to something or someone?
    - ☞ Family
    - ☞ Job
    - ☞ Museums and cultural centers
    - ☞ Urban area
    - ☞ Country, mountains, beach area
    - ☞ Friends
- Will you save time or money directly or indirectly from this change?

- What positive long-term outcomes can you see resulting?

    Examples: More accessible to a university so you can take courses part time; freed up to pursue a part-time job; time alone to think, read, write; spiritual awakening and discoveries; forced to make an overdue change.

- What good qualities have other people involved in your change displayed?

    Examples:

    ☞ My former husband will handle the selling of our home. I will be moving into my new home at 98 Maple Avenue.

    ☞ My employer, Rite-Way Electronics, has provided career placement and a generous three months of salary to help me succeed during this transition in my career.

Whether you are divorcing, retiring, or changing jobs, people are much more likely to seek you out and help you if you convey that you are helping yourself. Friends and acquaintances may dread contacting you if they fear they will hear a long list of complaints and whining. Show that you are forward thinking. People like to join the positive momentum of a person looking forward to the future.

STANDARD LETTERS RELATING TO LIFE CHANGES

Relaying a New Address

We wouldn't want to be out of contact with you—even for a little while. Our address has changed, and we wanted you to have it right away:

> 610 Cross Creek Pointe
>
> Marietta, GA 91201
>
> Phone: (555) 666-7777

We are enjoying our new home because <u>it is more convenient to our jobs.</u>
(we are near our elderly parents/the schools are wonderful here)

As you can tell, we wanted to send this so we could remain in touch with you.

Announcing a Divorce

This letter is to share with you some unhappy news about <u>Sam and me</u>.
(couple)

We are divorcing and wanted you to hear about this from us personally.

Reasons are not important; suffice it to say that the divorce is a reality

and will probably be final <u>in October</u>.
(in the spring)

Your friendship is, as always, valuable to me. That will not change.

<u>Sam is moving upstate to be closer to his company headquarters, but I</u>
(state generally who is moving where)

<u>will still be here.</u>

We appreciate your <u>thoughts</u> at this time. I hope my new life includes
(prayers)

more good times with you.

Announcing Retirement

You probably never thought this day would come, but I am retiring.

My career at <u>Georgia-Pacific</u> will officially end on August 18, 2000.
      (company name)

I have spent <u>twenty years</u> there.
      (many/five)

I am so looking forward to <u>days with my grandchildren and time for</u>
      (travel/time with Mary/volunteering at St. Joseph's)

<u>my freelance writing</u>.

Thank you for being a part of my life during these <u>twenty years</u>. I look
      (many/five)

forward to an interesting and fulfilling retirement.

Announcing a Serious Illness

As my <u>friend</u>, you have always been supportive. I feel I should continue
   (co-worker)

our habit of communicating openly with one another by sharing with

you that I have been diagnosed with <u>liver cancer.</u>
                              (state diagnosis with
                              no descriptive words)

As you might expect, I am making some adjustments to <u>my work</u>
                                        (my routine/
                                        my travel plans)

<u>schedule and diet.</u>

Also, I will be treated with <u>chemotherapy at Armada Cancer Center.</u>
                         (state any treatment or other things to expect)

<u>Dr. Kevin Jones know of an experimental drug that is very promising.</u>

My outlook is good and I plan to continue to enjoy our <u>friendship.</u>
                                        (great working
                                        relationship)

You can help most by <u>keeping an optimistic outlook with me.</u>
                  (prayers/assuming a business-as-usual
                  approach with me)

Thank you for your understanding. I just felt that you should know.

Acknowledging a
Friend's Serious Illness

When you shared with me recently that <u>you have cancer</u>, I could not
(you have been diagnosed
with a serious heart condition)

immediately express to you all that <u>was in my heart</u>. I care about you
(went through my mind)

and want to offer you my support.

You can count on me for <u>prayers and whatever else you need.</u>
(emotional support/an always-available
listener and friend/transportation to
your appointments)

Thank you again for sharing this news with me. It will help me be a

better friend to you as you experience your treatment. I look forward

to seeing your full recovery. In the meantime, you surely know that

you are not alone in this. I care.

 NOTE: *Seriously ill people, in general, appreciate your
acknowledging their illness. To pretend that nothing is
wrong is a type of burden to many patients. Use your
judgment to decide whether your friend would appreciate
a letter like this.*

CHAPTER

8

COMPLAINTS AND COMPLIMENTS

TIPS: Effective Complaining

•

Standard Letters of Complaint

•

Letters Acknowledging Good Service

•

Making Other Arrangements

- How do I get quick, efficient results?

- How can I be persuasive enough to get the company/person to see things my way?

- How do I express clearly exactly what my problem is?

TIPS: EFFECTIVE COMPLAINING

Remember that when you complain to an employee at a business you are complaining to a person who has no emotions about your situation—at the beginning. The employee only wants to do his job as quickly and easily as possible. Your goal is to make the task of giving you what you want as easy as possible for the employee.

If you lay the letter out as an action plan or a to-do list, the employee can go down the list easily to solve the problem and get it off his desk. When the employee handling your complaint sees your letter, he will see he can go through the list with no hassle. How do you write a letter like this?

- State clearly and simply at the beginning what you want: refund, new appliance, repair, etc.

- Use bullets to list the steps the company must take to give you satisfaction.

- Thank the employee in advance for the kind service you assume you will receive.

So many dissatisfied customers write lengthy, emotional complaint letters, but never specifically say what they want. Customers often think that it's glaringly obvious what the company needs to do, such as replace an appliance. Believe it or not, these companies often don't see it that way unless you say the obvious: "I want you to ship me a new Bagel Toaster, Model #4327, to replace the one that burned."

Companies are not mind readers. You will get what you want more often by taking your reader by the hand, so to speak, and leading him step by step through the process of making you once again a satisfied customer.

STANDARD LETTERS
OF COMPLAINT

Defective Product

Please <u>insert what you want</u>. To expedite this matter I have enclosed
(refund my payment of $140/
send me a new can opener—Model #230A/
repair my Aero bicycle)

<u>insert anything you have to send company</u>.
(the receipt/the name and phone number of the store/
the broken can opener)

Best business practices dictate that you cooperate with me under these circumstances. I have summarized the basis of my complaint below:
<u>Summarize clearly and exactly the problem with the appliance or service.</u>

Thank you for handling this problem for me. If you have any questions, you can reach me at <u>phone number, address, and all pertinent information needed to satisfy your request.</u>

For a longer letter:

One additional concern I want you to note in your files is that

<u>insert safety or other problems you feel should be reported.</u>
(danger to children or environment)

*P*lease send me a new *Aztec electric pencil sharpener, Model #13.* To expedite the matter, I have enclosed both the sharpener I purchased and a copy of my receipt. Best business practices dictate that you cooperate with me under these circumstances. I have summarized the basis of my complaint below.

I purchased the *Aztec sharpener #14A* on May 1, 1999. Fairway stores, where I purchased the *Aztec sharpener #14A,* offers refunds for only two weeks after date of purchase. The sharpener's motor burned out May 20, 1999, and I was no longer eligible for a store refund. The store manager informed me that many of these sharpeners have been returned with burned-out motors.

For this reason, I must insist that you replace this product with your *Model #13* instead of the troubled *Model #14A.* The new sharpener may be sent to me at:

44 Elm Street
St. Louis, MO 30004

One additional concern I want you to note for your files is that this motor problem could potentially cause an electrical fire. Since school children might be using this style pencil sharpener, I feel *Aztec* has a responsibility to contact other purchasers.

Thank you for handling this problem for me. If you have any questions, you can reach me at (555) 666-7777.

Request for Refund/Deposit Back

lease send me a <u>refund</u> in the amount of <u>$0.00</u> at your earliest
      (deposit)   *(amount)*

opportunity. The <u>refund</u> is due me because <u>state reason.</u>
            (deposit)   *(I did not use your service/*
                                                      I returned your tool rental)

According to best business practices, it is now up to you to expedite this

matter. I will look forward to a speedy return of my <u>refund.</u>
                                                                (deposit)

> *P*lease send me my deposit in the amount of
> $1,240.50 at your earliest opportunity.
> The deposit is due me because:
> - I fulfilled the terms of my lease on the apartment
>   at 200 Phillips Street.
> - I left the apartment in as good or better condition
>   than it was at the beginning of the lease. I paid
>   the professional cleaners you recommended to
>   do a final cleaning. Enclosed is a copy of
>   the cleaning bill.
>
> According to best business practices, it is now
> up to you to expedite this matter. I will look
> forward to a speedy return of my deposit.

Service Problems

Your help in solving the following service problem is needed:

<u>Insert a brief description of the problem.</u>
(Examples: Your cable service does not deliver The Mechanic's Channel clearly to my television set/ Your team of pool cleaners is not cleaning the drains of my pool as stated in your contract)

You can solve this problem by:

<u>Insert here, in bullets, exactly what you want to happen.</u>
- *Instructing your team to clean the drains on every monthly visit*
- *Checking to make sure that they do this for the next two months*

I appreciate the help you are willing to give in order to provide me with good service. I am hopeful that we will be able to work this out so that I can continue to be a customer of <u>company name</u>.

Your help in solving the following service problem is needed:

- *Each week, when your crew picks up my trash cans, several items of garbage fall out and are left on my lawn.*
- *I have spoken to your crew twice in the last month about this with no results.*

You can solve this problem by:

- *Requiring your crew to check for spilled trash at 201 Hatfield Drive.*
- *Personally checking up to make sure this is done on Thursday, February 21, 2000, my next pick-up date.*

I appreciate the help you are willing to give in order to provide good service. I am hopeful that we will be able to work this out so that I can continue to be a customer of Oscar's Garbage Service.

Reporting an Employee's Poor Service/Performance

Because you have an interest in retaining customers, I am writing to tell you of a problem I experienced with your business. It is my hope that you will be motivated to solve this problem, just as I was motivated to report this disappointing experience.

<u>Tim Rollins</u>, <u>a salesman</u> for <u>Salisbury's Men's Store</u>, is the employee
(employee (employee's (business name)
name)   position)

who is responsible for my dissatisfaction. To help you take steps to

remedy this poor service, I have summarized the problem below:

On June 1, 2000, I ran into Salisbury's to grab a last minute birthday gift for my father-in-law. For over twenty years I have received good, fast service from Salisbury's, and I expected the same service that day.

Perhaps because I had been doing yard work and was dressed in warm-ups, Mr. Rollins ignored me for thirty minutes. He waited on customers who had entered the store after I had. After all other customers had been served, he began folding sweaters and ignored me. I asked him for his help, and he unenthusiastically walked over to the suits with me. When I asked if he had anything in a lighter weight wool, he suggested I check Sears or K-Mart. Clearly, he thought I was not in an income bracket to afford to shop at Salisbury's. Mr. Rollins was unhelpful and uncooperative, and I walked out empty-handed.

What you might consider doing is <u>training Mr. Rollins in diplomacy</u>
(give me $25 gift certificate to apply to
the next suit I purchase)

<u>and informing him that many people with money don't wear it.</u>

Thank you for resolving this customer service problem.

....

NOTE: *The most effective letters will be addressed to the actual name of the owner or manager of the business. A phone call is all it takes to find out this name. If that proves impossible, address the letter to Owner/Manager.*

Verifying Delivery Time/Date

To assure that your delivery people have no problems with my delivery, I am writing with this request.

Please verify the delivery time and date for the <u>washing machine</u> that
(item purchased)
I purchased from <u>Garrison's</u> on <u>May 15, 2000</u>. I want to make sure
(business name) (date of purchase)
<u>that someone is here to open the door for you.</u>
(that someone will be here to sign for it/that all arrangements are made)

Please call me to confirm the following delivery information:

Item to be delivered:	Whirlpool Washer X14
Date of delivery:	May 25, 2000
Time:	9:00 A.M. to 11:30 P.M.
Address:	64 Mockingbird Circle
Verify by phone at:	(555) 666-7777

Thank you for your prompt response.

Delivery Is Unacceptable

You value customers and the business they bring you. I recently experienced a problem that was unacceptable to me as a customer. I hope, as a businessperson, you will also find it unacceptable.

Unacceptable Delivery

On Tuesday, March 16, 2000, a package from your company, Right Guard, delivered Burglar Alarm (#AK04) to me via Express Mail. On arrival, the alarm was broken, and no instructions were included explaining how I might send the damaged article back to you.
(Briefly summarize the problems with the delivery. Include dates, middlemen, delivery company names, and model numbers.)

Solution

To remedy this problem quickly, please send me a new Burglar Alarm #AK04 with instructions telling me how to return the broken alarm to you. Of course, the alarm and the postage would be prepaid by Right Guard.
(state precisely the solution you seek/state who is responsible for arrangements and costs)

It is my hope that you have a businesslike plan in place to take care of incidents like this. Accidents can happen. This gives you the opportunity to demonstrate the customer service that you advertise.

Incomplete Work—
Contractor/Service

I am writing in hopes of working out a problem that has arisen on the following job:

WORK ITEM: Hanging sheetrock - bath area

LOCATION: 2941 Glen Arden Drive
            Alto, California

CUSTOMER: Carey Haley

PHONE: (555) 666-7777

On <u>September 1, 1999</u>, I entered into an agreement with <u>Wall Wizard</u>
      (Date)   *(contractor/*
                                                                   company name)

<u>to install sheetrock for a new bath in my home.</u> <u>Your estimator</u> said
(task to be completed)   *(Darren Evans/*
                                                your foreman/your office)

that the work would be complete <u>within a month, which would have</u>
                                                   (state due date)

been <u>October 2, 1999</u>. It is now <u>October 15, 1999</u> and the job is not
                                             (Date)

complete. Please contact me within three business days to make arrangements to remedy this situation. Your failure to complete the work as agreed upon has resulted in costly problems to me, as well as <u>lost time and general inconvenience</u>. Your reputation is important to
(state any costs, tangible or intangible)

you, I am sure. I hope you will handle this promptly and professionally.

<u>For a longer letter:</u>

If not, I will be forced to <u>take measures to ensure that the work is completed.</u>
                                      (contact my attorney/cancel the rest of my contract/
                                      withhold payment for work not done)

Completing a Task/ Meeting a Deadline

To follow up on our <u>agreement</u> about the landscaping project, I thought
(earlier conversation)

I should write. Our <u>deadline</u> will soon be here, and I'm just verifying
(project's end)

with you that everything is on time and will be completed by <u>May 29th.</u>
(insert your deadline)

As usual, don't hesitate to call me if you have questions or needs. I'll do whatever I need to do to help meet our <u>agreed-upon deadline.</u>
(goal of May 5th completion)

LETTERS ACKNOWLEDGING GOOD SERVICE

Thank You for Good Service

Last Friday, while shopping in your boutique, I experienced superior
(night/month)   *(dining in your restaurant/*
browsing in the library/
having my car washed)

service. Such good service doesn't happen every day. I felt I should

pass my compliments on to you.

You might be interested to know that I was particularly impressed with

the dressing room attendant, who was discreet but helpful.
(the wait staff/the checkout desk clerk)

Thank you for such a good experience. With service like yours, I look
forward to returning.

Thanking Your Maid, Staff, Secretary, or Other Employee for Good Service

Your help is so valuable to me. I just want to let you know how much I appreciate all you do.

When I <u>see how organized the pantry is and how clean the windows are,</u>
(state a couple of examples of good work/see how smoothly this office runs)

I realize how special the work you do for me is. Thank you. You are a person I value, and I wanted to let you know.

Acknowledging Good Service of an Employee to the Owner/Manager

Acknowledging good service is a rare but welcome opportunity. Your

employee, <u>Tom Renfroe</u>, has given me the kind of service that deserves
    (employee's name)

acknowledgment. <u>Tom</u> sets <u>himself</u> apart by <u>offering suggestions</u>
    (employee's (herself)   *(describe the good service*
    name)   *you have received)*

<u>regarding the menu and by keeping my needs met without hovering</u>

<u>too closely.</u> He is always <u>polite but doesn't interrupt conversations as</u>

<u>some waiters do</u>.
(He exceeds what is required of him)

In a business such as yours, employees like <u>Tom</u> are a valuable asset.
    (employee's name)

He represents your <u>business</u> well and that attracts customers like me.
<u>(She)</u>   *(shop/garage)*

Thank you for a good <u>dining</u> experience.
    (customer service/shopping)

*A*cknowledging good service is a rare but welcome opportunity. Your employee, Jane Camden, has given me the kind of service that deserves such recognition.

Jane sets herself apart by handling my checkout from my dental appointments with efficiency and cheerfulness. She takes the initiative to offer to help me fill out the many complex forms that I must send to my insurer. She exceeds what is required of her.

In a business such as yours, employees like Jane are a valuable asset. She represents your practice well, and that attracts customers like me.

Thank you for a good experience.

MAKING OTHER ARRANGEMENTS

Cancelations

Please cancel my *Atlanta Journal* weekly subscription.
(Academy Theater Season Tickets)

We are moving and will no longer need a local paper. To help you close
(may or may not list reason for cancellation)

out my account, I have put together the following information for you:

ACCOUNT #:   11407

NAME: Polly Parton

ADDRESS: 376 Pollywood Drive

             Nashville, TN 11144

PHONE: (555) 666-7777

You should also know that I have received wonderful service during my
(terrible)

time with you as a customer.

Thank you for your help in closing out my account in an orderly

manner.

Arranging for Special Needs

Your <u>hotel</u> has a reputation for doing things well. I am writing ahead
(school/business)

to tell you of a special need I have. Perhaps with this advance notice,

neither you nor I will be inconvenienced.

On <u>March 4, 2000</u>, I will be <u>arriving for a two-week stay.</u> <u>I use a wheelchair</u>
  (list dates/times)   *(arriving at noon to speak*   *(state need/disability)*
                           in the West Point room)

and <u>will need all rooms and services to be wheelchair accessible.</u> To
                          (state needs)

ensure that things run smoothly, it would be helpful if you would

<u>send me a map of your floor plan.</u>
(send an attendant out to my car to help carry the equipment)

Thank you in advance for this service. Please call me at <u>(555) 666-7777,</u>
                                             (phone number)

to confirm these arrangements.

CHAPTER

9

CORRESPONDING WITH PROFESSIONAL PEOPLE

- How do I supply the information that professionals need from me?

- What is the most effective way to get a response from busy professionals?

- How can my letter get a faster response from a bureaucratic entity like the government or an insurance company?

TIPS: WHAT PROFESSIONALS NEED IN A LETTER

Most professionals, whether physicians or government employees, don't have a lot of patience for paperwork. From this characteristic you can identify two things that will help you write a letter to a professional:

- First, keep it short and to the point.

- Secondly, the professional probably won't deal with your letter personally. The fulfillment of your request will probably be executed by an assistant or a clerical person.

Now you have to look at the second issue. If a clerical person is assigned to respond to your letter and, you hope, your request, what does that clerical person need from you? Here are some things that you should include to help others deliver the results you want:

- Your name (and any maiden names or other relevant name changes)

- Names of all parties involved

- Exact dates related to the information you are requesting

- Any invoice numbers, admissions dates or other dates, or other numerical information

- Exact but simple statement telling precisely what you want

- Brief recap of previous letters sent, phone calls made, and so on— this is impressive if written as a timeline. A timeline is simply a list of events in chronological order. An example of a timeline appears on page 122.

- All information the reader will need to research the problem

- Information that tells how best to deliver an answer to you: name, address, phone number(s), E-mail, and voice mail. State if E-mail or voice mail answers are acceptable to you.

Busy professionals want to respond to your problem quickly so that they can move on. Make their job easy. Give complete and clear information. That way they don't have to waste time tracking down information you can give them in your letter.

 NOTE: *You don't have to include all the boring details in the body of your letter. It's much easier to put lots of facts into an attachment. An attachment is a separate sheet listing facts. The good news is that the facts don't even have to be in complete sentences in the attachment. See page 122 for an example of an attachment.*

TIPS: HINTS OF NEGATIVITY— LANDMINES TO AVOID

Even with the best intentions, we can still write a letter that hits our reader the wrong way. One word may provoke a hostile response. A particular way of phrasing may call up a bad association and alienate the reader.

Although no book can anticipate all the touchy subjects your readers may react to, here are a few pitfalls to avoid.

1. Never tell a reader what he "must, ought, or should" do. These words make some readers feel that you are condescending and bossy.

2. Avoid putting unpleasant things in writing. These documents live on. Conversations don't.

3. Avoid absolutes and hyperbole. Examples:

   • "This is absolutely the very last time."

   • "You have completed no work at all."

   • "I will never forget this for the remainder of my life."

   • Words like "obviously" and "clearly."

4. When you must write a letter about an unpleasant subject, avoid unpleasant phrases such as the following:

   • take issue with

   • you must agree

   • grossly overestimated

   • before it is too late

Requesting Records

Because you are <u>the physician who diagnosed my arthritis</u>, I am writing
*(state the reason this professional or this agency
is being contacted; example: the agency handling
my disability claim/the law firm who conducted
the closing on my home)*

to request <u>that you send my records to Dr. Aram Ritjik, a rheumatology</u>
*(state the request simply and briefly the first time; you can add
details in later sentences or in an attachment; examples: that
you send my records to Veterans Affairs in Washington/that you
mail me all the paperwork signed at the closing of my home
at 244 Atwater Creek, Hickory, GA 30303)*

<u>specialist</u>.

It is imperative that these records be sent as soon as possible because

<u>treatment cannot begin until Dr. Ritjik receives your records</u>.
*(I will have no income until this claim is processed/my attorney says that
these needed records are holding up the sale of my home)*

To help you expedite this request, I have put together <u>the following</u>
*(the information
on the attachment
enclosed.)*

<u>information</u>:

PATIENT'S NAME:	John Doe
ADDRESS:	223 Cade's Cove
	Marietta, GA 30064
HOME PHONE:	(555) 666-7777
WORK PHONE:	(555) 777-6666
DATES TREATED:	6/09/99
	6/18/99
	7/22/99
	8/30/99
DIAGNOSIS:	Rheumatoid Arthritis

Your help is needed in the effort to settle this matter.
*(relieve my pain/help me
conduct this closing with
the appropriate papers
from your firm)*

For a longer letter:

I know I can count on you to furnish the information requested since,

as a physician, you know how important it is to alleviate the pain as
*(you know how wasteful redoing these tests and evaluations would be/you are the
only agency tasked with helping a taxpayer like me who has become disabled/it was
our agreement that your firm would keep a set of the closing papers on record)*

soon as possible.

Thank you for facilitating this important process.

Requesting Records from a Government Agency

Because you are the agency responsible for keeping Cobb County property tax information, I am writing to request that you send me a copy of my 1998 tax bill stamped "paid."

It is imperative that these records be sent as soon as possible because there is an outstanding lien on my house for these taxes that is preventing my closing on the sale of my home. Since I paid the taxes, I need documentation from you that the lien was satisfied.

To help you expedite this request, I have put together the following information:

PROPERTY LOCATION: 690 Crossbow Creek
Auburn, CA 30103
TAX ID #:   81768409
OWNER'S NAME: Jimi Jones
LOT #:   241LGA
1998 TAX AMOUNT PAID: $2,800.41
DATE PAID: 11/12/98
SEND INFORMATION TO: Jimi Jones
P.O. Box 841
Auburn, CA 30103
or FAX to: (555) 666-7777

Your help is needed in this effort to settle the matter. I know

I can count on you to furnish the information requested since

this is part of the many services provided to taxpayers like me.

Thank you for facilitating this important process.

LETTERS RELATING TO PROFESSIONAL SERVICES

Reporting Mistakes

A recent mistake was made in your practice that you will want to be aware
(by your staff/by my
insurance company/
by me)

of and correct. On May 12, 2000, your physician's assistant, Mary North,
(cite date)   *(State name(s) of person(s) involved)*

gave a list of exercises to my eighty-year-old grandfather, James Dean.

These exercises were to be done at home. As you know, because

of the current pressure behind Mr. Dean's left eye, you had previously

recommended no bending from the waist. These exercises required

such bending.

Because of your professional standing, I am sure you will remedy this
situation. Please correct this error by helping us in the following ways:

- Modify the exercises for my grandfather, James Dean, patient ID
  #9126104

- Schedule us for another early morning appointment for Ms. North
  to go over the new exercises with Mr. Dean

- Arrange that the second appointment will not be charged to
  Mr. Dean, as a gesture of goodwill

Thank you for handling this as quickly as possible. A fast response is necessary since <u>these exercises are a key part of my grandfather's recovery</u>.
(state reason needed for fast turnaround)

You can respond to me in one of the following ways:

MAILING ADDRESS: John Farrow

22 Mill Street

Chinquapin, NY 11428

PHONE: (555) 666-7777

E-MAIL ADDRESS: farrow@znet.org

Your help is vital and greatly appreciated.

Reporting a Mistake
to an Accountant

A recent mistake was made by your firm that you will want to be aware of and correct. On April 14, 1999, your senior accountant, Ann Ryan, listed my child support payments as alimony on my 1998 tax return (Francine Rice; social security #200-500-8111, account #512A). This resulted in my overpaying taxes by $6,000.

Because you are such a well-regarded firm, I am sure you will remedy this situation. Please correct this error by helping in the following ways:

- Please re-do my 1998 tax return deleting the amount of child support payments erroneously included as alimony.

- As it was an error on the part of your staff, I am sure you will revise the return at no charge.

- Please mail the corrected return to me no later than Friday, May 15, 2000.

Thank you for handling this as quickly as possible. A fast response is necessary since I have lost the interest on this money for a year and don't wish to experience any more loss due to this mistake.

You can respond to me in one of the following ways:

CALL: Francine Rice
               (555) 666-7777

FAX: (555) 777-6666

Your help is vital and greatly appreciated.

Corresponding with an Attorney

As a <u>new</u> client, I am writing to you concerning <u>a case in which I am</u>
    (potential/   *(state your reason for*
    longtime)   *writing and your role)*

<u>the plaintiff</u>. Your firm is <u>handling my case through Randall Dupre</u>.
                                   (state the firm's role and pertinent names)

CLIENT NEED:

I need your help. <u>Over the last three months, I have received no calls or</u>
                   (state the problem)

<u>correspondence from Mr. Dupre. I have tried to reach him, but he does</u>

<u>not return my calls</u>.

Thank you for the integrity and professionalism your firm advocates. I look forward to working with you on this matter.

<u>For a longer letter:</u>

The enclosed attachment gives the history of the problem.

Here's a satisfactory plan for going forward:

1. Mr. Dupre calls me to update me on his progress
2. Your firm assigns a new attorney to take my case

ATTACHMENT

CASE: Jones vs. Smith

September 6, 1999	Called Mr. Dupre to ask about the progress of the case
September 10, 1999	Called a second time; left lengthy message with Marcia Martin
September 17, 1999	Third call; left voice mail message on Mr. Dupre's voice mail
October 10, 1999	Wrote a letter to Mr. Dupre asking about progress; sent it First Class
October 20, 1999	Re-sent the October 10 letter by certified mail
November 5, 1999	Visited your offices; Talked to Ezra Lighthorse about difficulties in contacting Mr. Dupre
December 6, 1999	Sent this letter to senior partner, Houston Snowden

CORRESPONDENCE RELATED TO HEALTH CARE AND INSURANCE

Corresponding with a Physician

As a <u>long-time</u> patient, I am writing to you <u>requesting a referral</u>.
(new/potential)   *(asking you to review these symptoms prior to our next appointment/asking you to consider adding my insurance company to your list of pre-approved providers)*

To help you review my case, I have listed the pertinent information below:

PATIENT NAME: Ashleigh Lane
PATIENT ACCOUNT #:   118064
PATIENT SINCE: 1989
RECENT DIAGNOSIS: Laryngitis
LAST APPOINTMENT: May 18, 2000

At your earliest convenience, please <u>refer me to an ear, nose, and throat</u>
                                      (state request)

<u>specialist in our area</u>.

<u>My laryngitis has become chronic, and I wish to see a specialist in</u>
                    (state request more specifically)

<u>chronic throat inflammation</u>.

Your profession entails your handling many things for your patients. I sincerely appreciate your <u>willingness to review your network of physicians and find the best throat specialist for me.</u>

Thank you for your help. The following information will help you respond to me as soon as possible:

PHONE: (555) 666-7777
E-MAIL: ashleigh@znet.org

Corresponding with a Hospital

I am writing to you concerning <u>a recent stay I had in your surgical ward</u>
                         (cite topic of letter and the department that is responsible)

at <u>Mercy Hospital</u>. One goal of hospital management is to conduct
  (hospital name)

business and patient care with high standards of quality. In my situation, the goal <u>definitely was not met.</u>
               (fell short in only one instance/was exceeded)

<u>The problem was that the anesthesiologist did not get the paperwork</u>
(briefly state the bad/good experience or other information you wish to convey)

<u>stating that I have low blood pressure.</u> As a result, <u>I had respiratory problems throughout surgery and consequently my recovery was more difficult.</u>

This situation <u>could have been life-threatening</u>.
(could have been costly/couldn't have been more pleasant)

The purpose of my letter is <u>to ask that you send a letter to the Incoming</u>
(state the result you want or say thank you)

<u>Patient Desk outlining the precautions they should take to insure this</u>

<u>never happens to another patient.</u>

For correspondence about a problem, add the following:

To help you investigate the problem, I have summarized below the

particulars of this event.

PATIENT'S NAME:	Tiffani Kitchens
PATIENT'S I.D. #:	11104
DATE OF SURGERY:	8/25/99
TYPE OF SURGERY:	Bletheroplasty
SURGEON'S NAME:	Dr. James Kildaire
ANESTHESIOLOGIST'S NAME:	Dr. Collier Hilton
DATE OF PRE-OP PROCESSING:	8/24/99
PATIENT'S ADDRESS:	777 Robin Lane
	Wilmington, DE 11140
PHONE NUMBER:	(555) 666-7777

Thank you for reviewing this letter and the situation. A timely response

will be greatly appreciated.

Reporting a Problem to an Insurance Company

As a premium-paying customer of <u>MetaLife Insurance</u>, I am writing to
(company name)

request some service to my account. To expedite an efficient handling of this matter, I have put together the following information for you:

INSURED'S NAME: John Paul Bondie

DEPENDENT (who experienced problem): Lisa Bondie (daughter)

ACCOUNT #:   88811

INSURANCE AGENT: Silver Industries

PHYSICIAN: Josh Bailey, Dermatologist
253 Reid Street
Evans, Montana 80061
(555) 666-7777

DATE OF PROBLEM: 12/12/00

To summarize, my daughter Lisa was referred to Dr. Bailey by our general practitioner, Drew Quincy, for a rash. Dr. Bailey was on your approved list of physicians, meaning that Lisa's bill should have been paid in full. I received a letter from your offices today stating that Dr. Bailey has been dropped from your approved list and that only half of our bill will be reimbursed by MetaLife. This is particularly disturbing since your logo was displayed at Dr. Bailey's office on the day of Lisa's treatment. Below your logo, these words were printed: "Approved Provider for MetaLife."

To correct this problem, I am requesting these steps:

- Reimburse the full amount of Lisa's treatment

- Require that Dr. Bailey take down the "Approved" sign and replace it with a sign stating plainly and in large letters that this practice is no longer on MetaLife's approved list.

- Consider providing a solution for families like us who get caught in your "approved list" changes. Even with the reimbursement, I must now take time off from work to get Lisa started with a different doctor, one who is on your "approved list."

Your cooperation is needed to rectify this situation without further difficulty. Thank you for a timely response.

CORRESPONDING WITH GOVERNMENT AGENCIES AND OFFICIALS

Requesting Assistance from a Government Agency

Your department, <u>Transportation and Communication</u>, has been tasked
(cite department name)

with serving <u>taxpayers</u>. Your help is vital in resolving the following
(veterans/children/
homeowners/voters)

situation:

PROBLEM:	The new Highway Connector 308 is proposed to run within 100 yards of my house at:
	353 Hardage Farm Lane,
	Sylvania, Rhode Island 30118
LOCATION:	Plat Book XYZ, Land Lot 60
HOMEOWNER'S NAME:	Matt Leroux
PHONE NUMBER:	(555) 666-7777

Why is this problem important?

First, my children and others play in this area. The proximity of a busy
(cite problem)

connector will surely create a danger. Second, the noise level will cause

a drop in my property value and that of the entire neighborhood. Tax

revenues will also drop. Finally, the connector can easily be rerouted

to the other side of Ajax Mountain, where neighborhoods are at least

three miles away. To resolve this, I expect a letter from your department
(cite your specific request)

stating you will not route the connector any closer than two miles from

my property.

For a longer letter:

I was told by Commissioner Engles that you were the person to contact.
(Mayor Campbell/the local head of the
Democratic Party/Customer Service)

Thank you for being efficient in handling this matter quickly. I cannot

overstate the seriousness of this matter.

Another letter requesting assistance:

In your position as city councilman, you are able to see that things are
(manager of the Sanitation Dept.)

done that will benefit our city and taxpayers like me. In the interest of

improving public safety, I am writing to request that you install a stop
(the Sanitation Dept.)   (add Christmas
tree recycling to
your services)

sign on Hardage Farm Drive, between Burnt Hickory and Crossfire Ridge.

Both taxpayers and our community in general will benefit from your support. Two of the positive effects you can help make happen are as follows:

- Avoid potential accidents where many small children play
  (Contribute to improving our environment)

- Help enforce a speed limit that is currently ignored
  (Give taxpayers a much appreciated service)

Thank you for taking this matter under advisement. My neighbors also appreciate your efforts.

Expressing Opposition—Politicians and Political Issues

Expressing strong opposition about an issue is the privilege and right
(support/ concerns)   *(a candidate)*

of a voting citizen like me. I am exercising that right by sending you this letter. I strongly oppose the funding of school construction through
(support)   *(State what/whom you support or oppose. examples: the nomination of Senator Hart/busing)*

lottery funds.

My reasons are many, but I will list my top three:

1. Historically schools have not benefited from lotteries over the long term, only the short term.

2. Lotteries increase crime.

3. Morally, I am opposed to gambling and am concerned about the example we will set for school children.

How can you help?

As a <u>senator</u>, you will be given the opportunity to vote <u>on this issue</u>.
 (city councilman)   *(for this candidate)*

Please <u>vote "NO" and represent the convictions of the people who</u>
        (state the specific action you want the reader to take)

<u>elected you</u>. Thank you again for the hours you devote to representing

the interests of <u>our district</u>.
                (state group)

....

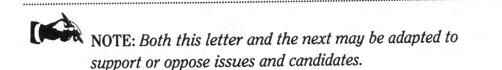 NOTE: *Both this letter and the next may be adapted to support or oppose issues and candidates.*

Expressing Support—Politicians and Political Issues

Voters have an exceptional opportunity this year. We can <u>give our support</u>
                                                          (oppose)

to <u>gubernatorial candidate John Wales</u> and truly advance <u>Cobb County</u>.
   (the new landfill)   *(the state of Georgia)*

For myself, I will lend my support, give my vote, and offer my resources

to make sure we <u>put this businessman and political leader to work for us</u>.
                (avoid putting this environmental hazard in our community)

After reviewing all the facts, I have many solid reasons to <u>support John</u>.
                                                           (oppose the landfill)

Here are my top three:

- John has voted "YES" on every bill funding school instruction since he has been in office.

- John's family has been a valued part of our community for twenty years, and his integrity is beyond question.

- John's success as a businessman gives him the savvy to create an effective budget that will keep taxes low.

How can you help?

As a <u>voter</u>, you will be given the opportunity to vote <u>for this candidate.</u>
(supporter)   *(on this issue)*

Please <u>vote for John Wales for governor on November 4th.</u>
        (state specific action you want the reader to take)

Thank you again for <u>taking your time to inform yourself about this</u>
                    (carefully considering this critical issue)

<u>candidate who could enhance our representation in state government.</u>

LETTERS TO WRITERS
AND SPEAKERS

Letters to the Editor

In the <u>May 5, 2000 edition of the *Atlanta Voice*</u>, <u>Max Gresham</u> stated that
(state issue, date, and title)   (state writer, if any listed)

"<u>the homeowners of Hart County have intentionally stunted the growth</u>
(list quote, if any)

<u>of that area to keep the area insular and to keep out outsiders.</u>" You should

be aware that this information is <u>false</u>. As an editor, you are responsible
(exaggerated/distorted/outdated)

for the integrity and validity of what the *Voice* prints. Please take steps
(paper's name)

to correct the information <u>given by Mr. Gresham</u>.
(in the May 5 article)

You should know that <u>Hart County is the fastest-growing county</u>
(state your facts)

<u>in Georgia. Also, Georgia is one of the top ten states when ranked</u>

<u>according to growth in the last five years.</u>

In short, I believe <u>that Hart's citizens have planned responsibly to</u>
(state your opinion)

<u>attract and maintain the very best developments, whether commercial</u>

<u>or residential.</u>

The article should <u>be corrected</u>.
(be retracted/
be amended)

Expressing a Compliment
to a Minister/Speaker

Your <u>sermon</u> on <u>kindness</u> really made an impression on me. I just had
  (speech)　　*(Sunday)*

to let you know how much I enjoyed it and how <u>on target</u> I thought it
  (astute/poignant/true)

was.

One part that I found <u>arresting</u> was <u>the story about Joseph</u>. Thank you
  (interesting)　　*(the pointers about how to*
  show acts of kindness)

for enlightening me. I look forward to hearing <u>your next sermon.</u>
  (you speak again)

TIPS: APPLYING FOR POSITIONS, JOBS, AND VOLUNTEER OPPORTUNITIES

Changes in our lives at any age can make a cover letter or other career-oriented letter a necessity. Here are just a few of the people who might need to write to friends or employees about openings and opportunities:

- A mother returning to the workplace after a few years at home with her children

- A teenager applying for his/her first job

- A middle-aged man who is making a career change due to a merger or downsizing

What Is Important in the Cover Leter of Your Resume?

If you know just a little bit about the company you are applying to, you can tailor your letter more effectively. These are a few general guidelines for writing the cover letter:

1. Your opening should say something specific about this job, this particular company, or the person to whom you are writing.

   Examples:

   - Filling the position of Marketing Director will lead you to consider a strong field of candidates. I offer to Acme Company the best possible credentials in that field.

- Employment at Acme Company has long meant career growth opportunities. Because I am interested in working for a company I can grow with, I am applying for the position of shipping clerk.

- Meeting with you last week about the sales position really brought me up to date about the business of energy consulting. I am more interested than ever in the position.

2. Highlight only a couple of the strong points of your background that apply to this job.

3. End with a statement of what you expect the next step to be: "I will call you on Friday to see what the Search Committee decided," or "I understand that you will notify me March 1 about your hiring decision."

4. Your cover letter should stress what you can do. That means you should use action verbs. Verbs are the words of movers and shakers. Verbs are the words of people who can successfully get a job done. Tell your future employer what you will accomplish for her if she chooses you for the job. Better yet, tell her the things you have already accomplished in your career:

- *Built* a twenty-person sales force to market a new product.

- *Achieved* or surpassed production goals for ten consecutive years.

- *Initiated* a plan to cut office expenses by 15% in one year.

- *Succeeded* in reducing office expenses by 18% in only seven months.

For a list of verbs to use in your cover letter/resume, see the next page.

Cover Letter and Resume Verbs

achieved	lowered	secured
boosted	managed	sold
built	maximized	supported
completed	minimized	surpassed
cut	progressed	turned around
improved	raised	upgraded
initiated	reduced	won

Cover Letter for a Resume— Version One

The position of <u>travel coordinator</u> that you are offering will require
      (name position)

<u>a variety of specific</u> skills, as well as more general qualities. With my
(strong computer/seasoned managerial/
outstanding interpersonal)

background <u>as a flight attendant</u>, I offer you both the skills and the
      (in computer science)

qualities you are seeking in a candidate.

You may be particularly interested in <u>my experience as a reservationist</u>
      (my degree in French)

<u>with Rich's</u>.

My resume is enclosed. You will find there further information qualifying me for this key position.

Thank you for considering my application. I look forward to the opportunity to interview with you at your earliest convenience.

Cover Letter for a Teenager Applying for Part-time Job— Version Two

The position of cashier that you are offering will require mathematical skills as well as other qualities. With my background as the concession-stand cashier at Oregon Park Baseball Field, I offer you both the skills and qualities you seek in a candidate. You may be particularly interested in my experience in closing out the register and balancing the receipts.

My resume is enclosed. You will find there further information qualifying me for this key position.

Thank you for considering my credentials. I look forward to the opportunity of interviewing with you at your earliest convenience.

Networking

Request for a Reference

Because I value your opinion, I am writing to ask you for a reference.

When I worked for you in the Tulsa office, you seemed to acknowledge
*(you lived next door to us/I serviced your
account/remind the reader of who you
are and how she knows you)*

my dedication to the job.
(potential/talent for writing)

If you could write a letter of reference for me, I would be very grateful.
You will find below the particulars that you will need to put together a
brief letter:

POSITION APPLIED FOR:	Sportswriter
COMPANY:	*Tulsa Star*
PERSON TO BE ADDRESSED:	John Stark, Employment Manager
ADDRESS:	6611 Wayfarer Boulevard
	Tulsa, OK 99488
JOB REQUIREMENTS:	Initiative, tolerance for long hours,
	writing skills, interpersonal skills

Thank you for considering this favor. I know you are busy. Your help
will be very valuable in this step in my career.

NOTE: *You may want to begin this letter with personal
comments if you know the reader well. Ask about the
reader's family, projects, and other interests.*

Asking for a Referral

I hope this letter finds you <u>enjoying a great third quarter</u>. My reason
(active in the market/busy with lots
of new customers/note something in
this line that refers to the reader's
business or job)

for writing you is to ask for your help. I would greatly appreciate your

giving me a referral to <u>the manager of Costco.</u>
(state to whom/what company
referral will be)

I want to <u>add them to my client list and present my software products</u>
(secure a management position with them)

<u>to their management</u>. A referral from you would be valuable in <u>getting</u>

<u>me an appointment to talk with the Costco people about carrying my</u>
(opening this door for me)

<u>line of software</u>. I will call you next week to get your thoughts, or you

can call me at (555) 666-7777.

Thank you for considering helping me. In any case, I am pleased to

have had this opportunity to touch base with you. I will let you know

if I <u>land the Costco account.</u>
(get an order/am hired)

CHAPTER
10

EVERYDAY CORRESPONDENCE

Letters to Those Close to Us—
An Effective Tool for Communication

•

Top Ten Reasons to Write Letters
to Relatives and Friends

•

Top Ten Components of a Great
Letter to a Relative

- How can I give my family the letters they want on a timely basis?

- How do I write every month/week and still sound newsy and interesting?

- Is there a formula for turning out a letter home quickly and easily?

- What sorts of things should I write about in day-to-day correspondence?

LETTERS TO THOSE CLOSE TO US–AN EFFECTIVE TOOL FOR COMMUNICATION

A parent finds a letter from an adult child in the mailbox. A college student finds a brief but encouraging note waiting at the dormitory. An old friend receives a letter after not hearing from another friend for many months. What elation and affirmation these moments bring. A letter can bring joy, fill an empty spot in the heart, and generate love and appreciation. Few tasks we undertake yield so much for so little time.

Why Don't Family and Friends Write More?

If we get such great results from writing to family and friends, why do we procrastinate? You may feel that letters demand too much thought and time. Using the form letters in this chapter can remedy that. Simply update the letter each month or each week. Fill in the different events or observations that apply. Your letter will write itself.

Why Are Letters the Best Form of Communication with Some Friends and Relatives?

The following are some surprising reasons why letters may be preferable to conversations in some situations.

TOP TEN REASONS TO WRITE LETTERS TO RELATIVES AND FRIENDS

1. You can choose the right words for the person, the situation, and your feelings.

2. Fewer misunderstandings can occur when you put plans and events in writing.

3. Emotions may color what people hear in a conversation. Expressing yourself in writing increases both your objectivity and that of the reader.

4. You may feel freer to reveal thoughts and feelings in a letter.

5. Others can't interrupt you when you write a letter. Even in the best relationships, one person often monopolizes the conversation and interrupts the other. A letter helps solve that problem.

6. Believe it or not, some people are embarrassed to say good things to another person face to face. A friend may have difficulty saying things like the following:

   - I love you

   - You were kind to me

   - You are a person I admire

   Letters help people express tenderness and intimacy in a "safer" venue.

7. You have a record of what you said in case misunderstandings arise later.

8. Letters from friends and family are often treasured and collected. They can even become a history of a family or a friendship.

9. Letters help you negotiate with family members rationally. You can clearly delineate what you want to change. The letter gives the other person time to compose a constructive response. Do you want to work out west this summer instead of staying with the family at the lake as you have always done? Write a loving letter telling of your excitement, your hopes, all the benefits of this change in family tradition for you. Say that you value the family time spent in past years. Appreciate what a disappointment and adjustment this will be for your family. THEN, ask for the family's understanding and support of your plans to spend the summer in the west.

10. Letters make some people creative. As you write, you create a word picture. You piece together your thoughts and weave something new.

Haven't Seen You in a While

Since I haven't seen you in a while, I thought I'd write. I'm sorry we haven't kept in touch, but maybe we can catch up soon. Are you still scouting for a new job?
*(attending cooking classes/working
with that difficult supervisor/working
out regularly/dating the accountant)*

Things haven't changed much with me. I still write in the mornings
*(manage the same department/
am working on my campaign
for city council/like to paint/
play my music loud and drink
too much coffee)*

and go to my second job in the afternoons. One thing new is that I've moved my office downtown.
*(I'm on a diet/I am enjoying playing
bridge these days/I'm seeing a psychologist)*

For a longer letter:

Let's touch base more often. I could E-mail you from the office.
(meet you halfway for lunch)

Is that convenient for you? Any suggestions?

Haven't Heard from You Lately

It's been too long since we <u>talked</u>, so I'm writing to get back in touch.
(wrote/got together)

When I last heard from you, you were starting <u>a new job and Missy was</u>
(insert your activities in the following blanks)

<u>beginning art lessons</u>. How are the <u>job</u> and the <u>lessons</u> going?
(tennis)   *(job search)*

As for me, I am still <u>volunteering in the library</u> and <u>working at the</u>

<u>hospital on weekends</u>. Life is <u>good</u>, but I still miss our <u>talks</u>. Could
(satisfactory/okay)   *(correspondence)*

we plan to <u>meet halfway in Cartersville for lunch one day</u>?
(start writing once a month again)

Thinking of You

You have been on my mind, so I thought I'd write. How are you? I'd love to know <u>how that blind date went</u>.

(how that problem at work was resolved/how your cat is adjusting to the new apartment)

As for me, I <u>have doubled the size of my department in the last year</u>

(put your news here; it can be a sentence or several pages)

<u>and am very busy.</u>

If you have the time, I would enjoy hearing from you. We have had some good times together. Do you remember when <u>we worked together on</u>

(you first moved to Dallas/ we had to leave the theater we were laughing so hard)

<u>our first project</u>?

Let's get caught up soon.

TOP TEN COMPONENTS OF A GREAT LETTER TO A RELATIVE

So many things go into a good letter home. Here are the top ten components. You should:

1. Express your love, fondness, homesickness, or other emotion.

2. Express concern for whatever *they* talked about last (sinus headache, new roommate, crabgrass, noisy neighbor).

3. Ask rhetorical questions about what is going on in their lives.

   Examples: How's your job? How is that demanding boss? Are you still dating the teacher? How is your yard coming along?

4. Offer newsy tidbits from your life.

   - Where have you been? Sports activities, parties, dates, visits with friends, museums and other cultural activities.
   - What have you accomplished? Selected for committees, finished a major project, elected treasurer of homeowner's association, given a raise.
   - What funny or touching stories can you tell? Locking yourself out of the car while it's running, finding that your toddler has painted the front end of your car, finding the missing hamster in your briefcase in a staff meeting.

5. Note any changes in your life.

6. Mention good memories that have occurred to you lately. What triggered them?

7. If you live in a different community, describe how it differs from home: Rodeos? May Day? Traditions? Architecture? Rollerblading in streets? Street performers? Climate? Weird things?

8. Give the reader something to look forward to: "I hope to see you in the spring; I'll call you next week."

9. End with an expression of fondness or love.

10. Don't procrastinate! Write now!

Letter Home—Version One

I hope this letter finds you <u>fit and healthy</u>. This is the time of year
(as energetic as ever/as knee-
deep in the projects you love
as ever/happily planting your
spring garden/victorious in your
battle against the groundhogs)

when I know that you usually <u>have hay fever</u>. Knowing this, I hope
(plant your garden/get extra busy)

you can <u>take extra care of yourself</u>.
(enjoy the time outside/pace yourself)

As for me, I have occupied myself in several ways. <u>I'm training a new</u>
(state what you have
done lately)

<u>staff member at work. That's time-consuming. I'm trying to get my</u>

<u>sewing room organized. That's challenging. I'm working to adjust</u>

<u>to having Joshua living at home since his college graduation. That's</u>

<u>probably futile.</u>

Life is pretty <u>full</u>. I look forward to <u>my vacation in two months.</u>
(hectic/challenging/   *(retirement/my weekends/seeing*
wonderful/tough)   *you for Passover)*

Take care and keep in touch.

Letter Home—Version Two

No one knows how <u>much I miss you</u>. Though a lot has happened, I
(homesick I am/busy two kids
can keep a person/much I crave
Southern Fried/different Atlanta
is from L.A./busy this campus
stays almost around the clock)

always have time to <u>miss you</u>.
(think good thoughts of you/
drop you a line each month/
appreciate what you have
done for me/remember what
great parents I have)

My <u>month is</u> the usual. I <u>took both kids to the dentist, got the car</u>
(weeks) (are)   *(list several things you have done)*

<u>repaired, served at the anniversary party for Little Ed's school, and</u>

<u>went to a company barbeque with Big Ed</u>. So far, things are shaping

up to be pretty <u>busy</u>.
(routine/scary/
depressing)

What about you? Have you <u>completed the addition to your house?</u>
(done anything interesting/had a good month/
changed anything more drastic than the oil
in your car)

I look forward, as usual, to hearing from you.

Travel—Letters to Friends and Relatives

What a(n) <u>relaxing</u> place this is. I wish I could describe <u>how beautiful</u>
      (exotic/charming/
      interesting)

<u>the local waterfalls are.</u>
(how rested we are/this picturesque
town/the festive atmosphere)

Your week, I hope, is going well. How is your <u>allergy problem?</u>
                                      (baby adjusting to
                                      solid foods/mother
                                      after her surgery)

We should be <u>returning on May 29th.</u> The pace has been <u>just right.</u>
      (here at least two more weeks/   *(too fast for me/*
      moving on to Genoa soon)   *lively)*

I will have much to share with you when I see you.

Take care of yourself and <u>that motley crew you work with.</u>
                       (those high-energy children/John/
                       your sweet family)

CHAPTER

11

ON BEHALF OF CHILDREN

Writing on Behalf of Your Children

•

TIPS: Why Write Frequently?

•

Letters Relating to School

•

Letters About Illness, Medication, and Attendance

•

Acknowledging Accomplishments and Milestones

- How do I convey warmth and appreciation to school employees for all that they do?

- Teachers read many notes daily. How can I avoid wasting their time?

- How do I make a positive impression on principals and teachers?

- How do I make sure school employees explicitly follow directions regarding my children?

WRITING ON BEHALF OF YOUR CHILDREN

If you have children, much of your correspondence will be on their behalf. You must write notes or letters if they are ill, change schools, start school, finish school, and everything in between. It is also a good policy to write notes about little things that happen, even if good manners don't require a note or letter.

TIPS: WHY WRITE FREQUENTLY?

If the only time your school hears from you is when you need something or there is a problem, you will not be a very effective advocate for your child. Take every opportunity to acknowledge any positives that you notice:

- Teacher retirement
- Graduation
- Achievement of another child
- Awards, achievements

Notice that even the "Letter of Concern" on page 156 leads with a compliment.

Also, take the time to write instead of just calling when you need something. You want your directions and needs to be communicated accurately. So often, school volunteers and staff don't convey your requests verbatim to teachers, principals, and counselors. If you write a note or letter, your exact request is passed along—complete with your polite and friendly manner of asking.

LETTERS RELATING TO SCHOOL

Letter of Concern

I appreciate all you do, as <u>principal</u>, on my child's behalf. One thing I've
(teacher)

especially appreciated is <u>the orderly and clean facility you provide</u>.
*(the focus on academics at Sprayberry/
your caring attitude)*

One thing that does concern me, however is <u>the low standarized test</u>
*(the recent fights in the parking
lot/the change to the semester
system)*

<u>scores reported by the *Doubleday Journal* on Tuesday</u>. It would be

helpful to me as a <u>parent</u> if you could <u>call me with more information.</u>
(guardian)   *(advise me on how to raise Johnny's
scores/meet with me next week to
discuss this/call on Thursday or Friday
morning, if either is convenient for you)*

Thank you again for the many things you do as <u>principal</u>. With your
*(a teacher/
superintendent)*

help, I'm sure we will <u>begin to see some improvement in this situation.</u>
*(be able to help our students deal with this/
solve this problem)*

Entering/Applying to Schools

I am <u>submitting my child's application</u> for admission to The <u>Walker</u>
  (attaching information about Stephen)

<u>School</u> for your consideration. Two <u>strengths</u> make Walker my choice:
  (achievements/qualities/facets/programs)

- <u>High ratings on the IOWA Basic Skills</u>
  (outstanding music program/diversified academics)

- <u>Individual attention to student needs</u>
  (your programs for learning-disabled children/your preveterinary program)

What can Walker expect from my child (me)?

- <u>A well-rounded parent participant and volunteer for all activities</u>

- <u>A focused student with a proven history of high grades</u>

Substitute your own accomplishments above.

(Examples: winner of Truett Scholarship Award/an accomplished leader who captained the swim team/member of the prestigious Gotham Chorus/honor roll student for three consecutive years)

<u>Optional</u>

Your help with the following tasks would be so valuable:

- Please send applications for financial aid

- Please send your projected tuition costs for next year

Thank you for taking the time to help my child (me).

STUDENT INFORMATION
Date
Address
Phone Number:

Name(s): _____

Age: _____   Birthdate: <u>00/00/00</u>   SSN#: ____-__-____

(May have more than one student applying. List second child's info here.)

Last School Attended:

Grades Completed:

Grade/Program Applying for:

> *(three-year-old preschool/middle school grades 6–8)*
> *(For two children, list on separate lines:*
> *- Tyler Johnson will be entering second grade*
> *- Tessa Johnson will be entering seventh grade)*

Academic Accomplishments:

> *(For a preschooler, knowing one's ABCs is an*
> *accomplishment. Winner of fourth-grade county-*
> *wide spelling bee. Be creative here. Be sure to list*
> *honors.)*

Extracurricular Activities:

> *(sports/leisure activities/church/neighborhood/*
> *professional/civic organizations)*

Additional Information:

Report Cards

Thank you for all you do as <u>John's</u> <u>chemistry</u> teacher. I am writing in
                (student's name) (subject)

response to <u>John's</u> recent report card. I am <u>concerned about</u> the
     (student's name)   *(interested in)*

following:

- Steps we can take to improve/maintain this grade
- The role homework versus tests plays in computing the grade
- The factors contributing to the low grade
- Tutors or other means of helping Johnny
- Setting an appointment with you to discuss Johnny's progress
- How we can challenge a strong student like Johnny

Replace the above concerns with a list of your own concerns.

With your support and ours, we look forward to <u>John's</u> ending the
                                         (student's name)

<u>year</u> on a successful note.
(quarter/semester)

Behavior Problems

I appreciate your contributions as <u>Carolyn</u>'s teacher. Please help me
(student's name)

work with <u>Carolyn</u> to improve her <u>problem with talking in class.</u>
(student's name)   *(work habits/study skills/impulsiveness/
tendency to argue/conflicts with another
classmate)*

You could help me greatly by <u>meeting with me next week.</u>
*(making a list of overdue assignments/calling
and describing the problem incidents to me/
moving Carolyn to another desk)*

Please let me know what you advise me to do to help.

Volunteering

As a supporter of <u>Huey School</u>, I would like to volunteer my services.
(the Booster Club/your fundraiser)

You may find me useful as a <u>library helper.</u>
*(as a telephone solicitor/as a helping hand to
decorate the gym for dances/when you need
bookkeeping help/in assisting young children
in the preschool classes)*

<u>For a longer letter:</u>

You can schedule me for any task you need. My schedule is most open
for this volunteer work <u>in the mornings.</u>
*(anytime but Tuesdays/on Wednesday and Friday
afternoons/if you call ahead so I can schedule it)*

Thank you for the opportunity to serve in such a worthwhile cause.
Thank you, also, for all the work you do on behalf of the children.

LETTERS ABOUT ILLNESS, MEDICATION, AND ATTENDANCE

Illness/Missed Class

Unfortunately, <u>Houston</u> has missed <u>three days of school</u> due to <u>the flu.</u>
    (child's name)   *(English class)*   *(brief name of illness— no lengthy descriptions)*

Thank you for helping him catch up on his work. Please send home with him any class work that he may have missed.

As usual, I appreciate all you do for my child.

Everyday Needs—Notes to Teacher/Nurse

<u>Clark</u> is looking forward to enjoying this school year in your class. We
(student's name)

will need your help in one important way. <u>Every day, Clark must take</u>

<u>his asthma medication with his lunch. I am bringing you a month's</u>
(explain situation and what you expect to be done/explain how you will help)

<u>supply on Monday</u>.

Thank you for helping us. If you have any questions, please call me at (555) 666-7777.

Special Needs

My <u>daughter</u> needs your help in meeting a special need. My child's
(nephew/stepson)

name is <u>Jamie Stone</u>, and she will <u>be entering your school in the fall.</u>
(child's name)
(state child's relationship to the reader/
be attending your camp in the summer/
is in your fourth period class)

<u>Jamie</u> will require that <u>insulin shots be administered to her in the</u>
(state need/snacks in the midmorning and midafternoon
due to her hypoglycemia/to be dismissed five minutes
early each day to go to the high school for an advanced
math class)

<u>morning and afternoon. She will need your staff nurse to administer</u>

<u>these shots.</u>

We realize the extra effort this will take and appreciate your help.

We look forward to a good experience <u>at The Westminister School.</u>
(at Whileaway Camp/
in your history class)

ACKNOWLEDGING ACCOMPLISHMENTS AND MILESTONES

Teacher/Principal Retirement

After <u>thirty-six years</u> of teaching, you certainly have many <u>fans</u>. You
(so many years/   *(memories/admirers/*
decades)   *wonderful experiences)*

leave behind a rich legacy of <u>knowledge and learning</u>. You have always
       (caring and instruction/academic
       lessons and life lessons)

been admired for <u>your commitment to quality instruction</u>.
      (your nurturing kindness/your hands-on style
      of teaching/your creative approach)

As you go forward into retirement, I wish you well.

<u>For a longer letter</u>:

May this be yet another fulfilling time in your life.

Acknowledging Achievement of Another Child (Written to Child)

When you recently <u>won the spelling bee</u>, you accomplished something
(were accepted to Princeton/
made honor roll/were chosen
for the choral group)

wonderful. Achievements like this should be acknowledged. That's why I am writing you this letter.

I just want to say "Congratulations," "Keep it up," and "Best of luck in the future." You may have heard these before, but I want you to know how sincerely I mean them. You are a very special person.

End of Year/Graduation (To Teacher)

As we approach <u>graduation</u>, I wanted to let you know just how much
(the end of the year)

your <u>history class</u> has meant to me. It's teachers like you who make
(help/support)

school a <u>memorable</u> experience.
(worthwhile/challenging/dynamic/
enriching/life changing/constructive)

<u>For a longer letter:</u>

One thing I'll always remember is <u>the day you had us role-play the</u>
(the first day you met with us/your
lectures/the great books you have
recommended)
<u>surrender of General Lee.</u>

Thank you for all you have done for me and for many other students.

End of Year/Graduation
(To Student)

You are the kind of student who <u>establishes a benchmark for everyone</u>
(excels/will achieve much in life/will do
well long after graduation/brings joy/
brings laughter to all who know you)

<u>else</u>. As we face <u>the end of the year</u>, I feel I must tell you <u>how you have</u>
(graduation)

<u>impressed me this year</u>.
(how much you've meant to me/
what a great future I feel you have/
that I think you're a fine artist)

I wish you all the best in the future. You have enriched <u>our lives</u> just
(our school/
our art program)

by being yourself.

Noticing Something Positive

I noticed that <u>Sprayberry had ten National Merit Scholars this year</u>.
(cite the positive/you've renovated the reception area/Sprayberry has
received a grant for new computer software)

This is just one of many good things happening at our school. Thank

you for making <u>Sprayberry</u> such a fine school for my <u>son</u> to attend.
(name of school)   *(granddaughter/foster child)*

I appreciate all you do for the education and development of the students.

Parent's Word of Encouragement

Although I have been proud of you for many things, I recently found a
new reason to admire you. Your <u>perserverence during a difficult time</u>
*(winning the Academic Trophy/kindness
to the exchange student)*

has given me yet another reason to be especially proud of you.

I love you and always will. Even if you had never accomplished a great
feat or won any awards, I would love the person you are. There is so much
about you that I value and care about. I love you just for being you.

Still, I wanted to take a moment to acknowledge to you what <u>effort this</u>
*(a creative
talent you
have)*

<u>took</u>. You are a person I respect very much.

CLUBS
AND OTHER
ORGANIZATIONS

TIPS: Diplomacy, Enthusiasm, and Inspiration:
Requirements of a Volunteer's Letter

•

Committees, Clubs, and Organizations

•

Volunteering and Volunteers

•

Requests and Invitations

- How can I be effective in urging people to give time and money to our cause without seeming pushy?

- How can I convey the appreciation and respect I have for the volunteers who give generously of themselves

TIPS: DIPLOMACY, ENTHUSIASM, AND INSPIRATION: REQUIREMENTS OF A VOLUNTEER'S LETTER

The toughest sale in the world is to get people to give their time or resources in nonpaying volunteer service. If you are active as a volunteer, you know we are constantly asking members and nonmembers to give, give, give:

- Work on committees
- Work in a concession stand, serve as a docent, clean up after events
- Donate products or services for fundraising
- Accept a leadership position that requires a sacrifice of time
- Give up an evening or a Saturday to help your organization

You may have had difficulty thinking of the right way to ask others to give. The form letters in this chapter will help you with the phrasing. What if you are the person who is asked to give? Just as difficult as asking others to give is being in the position of being asked. How do you decline yet make the asker understand the high regard that you have for her, her organization, and the task you declined?

On the other hand, if you accept, how do you convey the enthusiasm and energy you will bring to the job? An acceptance of a volunteer position or task can sound one of two ways:

- Oh, all right, I guess I'll have to do it since I've been put on the spot.

OR

- Thank you for giving me an opportunity to bring my expertise and energy to this important task. You honor me by choosing me for the talents and resources I will bring to this job.

Which one makes you sound like a winner?

Diplomacy

One quality your volunteer letters must always display is diplomacy. Everyone in the Garden Club may know that the treasurer had to step down because she had gotten the books in such a tangle. Still, you do not put any of these negatives in writing. Refrain from the temptation to say: "Our books are in such disarray and you are the person to fix them." Instead, say: "Your accounting background and habit of doing all things with excellence are just two of the assets you bring to the role of treasurer."

Accentuate the positive. No need to mention the negative.

Enthusiasm

Volunteerism is a great institution, but the pay is lousy. People work together in a volunteer capacity for different reasons than they work for their employers and families. A few of those reasons include the following:

- Fellowship and fun with other adults
- A feeling of doing something that is worthwhile and humanitarian in nature
- A need to be appreciated
- A feeling of being part of a volunteer "family" or team
- A compelling desire to serve others in need

For all of the above reasons and more, it helps when people feel good about what they are doing. Whether you are a leader or a pair of hands on a job, be consistent in showing your enthusiasm for what you are doing:

- State your excitement about the project and the people you work with.
- Give accolades and ataboys—not only to those who work for you, but to leaders who may not get much feedback for the good job they are doing.
- A little rah-rah talk along the way helps revive the energies of others when a project drags out or requires long hours. Compliment, praise, and sympathize. Acknowledge long hours, time away from home, costs of all kinds, and creative input.
- Find milestones and little things to celebrate. Find excuses to congratulate people. Acknowledge the tiniest success. When people work hard for no monetary reward, they need to be rewarded in other ways. If you see anything done well or any task completed, write a note. This is the reward some volunteers treasure. Listed below are some examples of milestones or tasks you could acknowledge in a note or letter.

    Preliminary project approval is gained by a government agency, the bank, a committee

    An initial presentation announcing a project goes well

    A first draft is completed

    Something needed for the project is purchased: land, equipment, a license, advertising, materials

    A model, prototype, or first production item is finished

An event along the way is successfully completed: a fundraiser, an announcement party, a press conference, a meeting

The organization gives a project a vote of confidence, allocates budget dollars, or acknowledges the project

Statements that show your enthusiasm get others enthused. Savvy leaders know that getting people pumped up increases energy, production levels, hours voluntarily worked, and the chances of success. Here are a few examples that express and generate excitement:

- Thank you for making the art show a success.
- No one could have done it better.
- You accepted a difficult task, and you succeeded.
- I noticed how well you handled crowd control.
- Your talent for creating lovely table displays was evident everywhere.
- Thanks to your business sense, our accountant says our books are in great shape.
- Much of the credit for our receiving the grant goes to you.
- No one will ever know the countless hours you put into the booth display, but we, nevertheless, appreciate all you did.
- You worked hard and the results were magnificent!
- We won the committee's full support thanks to your lucid presentation.

Inspiration

The greatest leaders often motivate people by the sheer force of their personalities. These leaders are personally inspiring. Others motivate volunteers by reminding them of the righteousness or beauty of a cause or goal.

In either case, inspiration is a key ingredient of any document to or from a volunteer. Here are a few items to include if you want to inspire others as you write a letter as a volunteer:

Restate the great need:

- There is no art museum within one hundred miles of our town.
- Children are hungry and deprived.
- We must improve the future of our children by improving their education and their school.
- What if Clara Barton or Florence Nightingale had said "No"?
- How many people will fall prey to this disease before we agree to work together to find a cure?
- If our children don't have a safe recreation center for basketball and other games, have you thought about the less desirable activities they might join in?
- We have an opportunity to make a difference, save lives, and turn this situation around.

How does this apply to the response letter when you are being asked to volunteer?

- Tell a committee chairperson that you accept because you want to play a role in bringing art to the West Cobb community.
- Agree to loan a painting because you want other Southerners to realize the impact the work of Menaboni had on botanical art.
- Emphatically say yes to host a fundraiser because, in good conscience, you must do your part to feed hungry children in the Sudan.

Take the ideas given to you in this chapter and couple them with the form letters that follow. The results will be dynamic. Not only will the people in your organization be more motivated, you will have won their respect and support.

COMMITTEES, CLUBS, AND ORGANIZATIONS

Invitation to Serve on a Committee

You have been recognized for <u>your volunteer efforts on behalf of the</u>
(long time service to our school/church/
your dedication to our music program/
your culinary talents)

<u>children of Cobb County</u>. On behalf of <u>The Junior League of Cobb</u>
(The First Presbyterian Church)

<u>County</u>, <u>I am</u> making a request that <u>I</u> hope you will thoughtfully
    (we are)   *(we)*

consider. Please join us as a member of the <u>Cookbook Committee</u>
(the Choir Guild)

for <u>2000–2001</u>. We feel our committee could greatly benefit from
(the next six months)

your <u>experience</u>.
(talents/expertise/
formal training)

For a longer letter:

The duties are <u>varied</u>. For the most part, you will be asked to do the
    (limited/few)

following:

- Help make decisions about future projects
- Organize and delegate work to our many volunteers
- Meet monthly with the committee

We hope that you will serve on this important committee. One of our
(I)

goals is to raise more than $10,000 in profits next year to donate to the
                    (fund the Bell Choir/provide a reception for the volunteers at Grady Hospital)

Children's Academy. If you want to join us as a member, please attend

a meeting at Jo Marley's home at 10:00 A.M. on March 25, 2000.
(please call me at (555) 666-7777)   (time)   (date)

Invitation to Chair a Committee

Leadership styles vary, but there is always the right kind of leader for

each project. You have been recognized as the person best suited to
    (committee/task)

chair the new Technology Committee for the Marietta Men's Club.
                                    (club name)

Your skills are particularly suited to this job because of your long-time
(experience/abilities)

interest in computers. Please accept this role as our new leader.
(your years of service/
your military training)

Your time and service will be greatly valued. Please call me at

(555) 666-7777, at your earliest convenience, to let me know what

you have decided.

Declining/Accepting a Position on a Committee, Board, etc.

Your invitation to join <u>the Steering Committee</u> both honored and
(the Board of Directors of St. Stephen's School)

pleased me. It is with <u>great pleasure I accept</u> this important role in
(regret I must decline)

our <u>Kiwanis Club</u>. My decision to <u>accept</u> is primarily motivated by
*(church/club)**(decline)*

<u>my desire to launch more projects on behalf of underpriviledged children.</u>
*(my family duties, which have recently increased/my previous commitment
to the volunteer work I have started at the Elizabeth Shelter)*

Thank you for giving me this wonderful opportunity. I value

our <u>Kiwanis Chapter</u>, and I appreciate your invitation to join.
(our parish members)

Invitation to Join a Club or Organization

With great pleasure, <u>I</u> would like to extend to you an invitation
 (we)

to join <u>The Commerce Club</u>. Our <u>organization's</u> purpose is to
 (club name)   *(club's)*

<u>provide a forum and a network for our community's business leaders.</u>
(provide activities and civic projects for women in Cobb County)

<u>The Commerce Club</u> recognizes <u>your success in our local business</u>
 (club name)   *(your civic leadership/your investment
                                 in our community)*

<u>community</u>. For this and many other reasons, we hope you will join

us as a new member.

<u>For a longer letter:</u>

If you accept our invitation, <u>please join us at a new member reception</u>
                              *(say what the next step is/please fill out the
                              enclosed application)*

<u>at the Marietta Country Club at 7:00 P.M., Friday, May 14, 2000.</u>

Thank you for considering this opportunity to join us.

Thank You for Serving
a Club or Organization

You have given generously of <u>your time, your energy, and your talents</u>
(three years of hard work/your expertise
and talents)

to <u>the Hospitality Committee of the Carriage Hill Homeowners</u>
(Boy Scout Troop 54/AARP)

<u>Association</u>, and <u>we</u> would like to thank you for all you have done.
(I)

You are a valued and respected member of our group.

<u>We</u> especially want to recognize you for <u>your work in improving the</u>
(I) *(your successful fundraising efforts)*

<u>pool area</u>. Many will benefit because you invested your time to help.

<u>Our</u> sincere appreciation for your service is extended to you for all you
(My)

have done. Thank you on behalf of <u>all the members.</u>
(the Executive Committee)

Addressing Divisiveness
in an Organization

Sometimes to solve a problem, the problem must first be acknowledged. This letter is to acknowledge that we are experiencing differences of opinion about <u>the decision to purchase new land for a neighborhood</u>
(whether to finance the Indian project)

<u>playground</u>. <u>My</u> primary purpose, however, is to urge you to view this
(Our)

friction as communication rather than as a stalemate.

With a membership of so many intelligent and accomplished people, many views and strong feelings are to be expected. Our group would not be the dynamic and interesting group it is without these differences.

Whatever the outcome is, I ask that we focus for the next few <u>weeks</u>
(months)

on working together. Please remember that this is only one <u>decision</u>
(project)

and that we have many other things in common that are positive.

<u>I</u> ask that whether or not you agree with the final decision on this
(We)

one matter, you continue to support this organization and your fellow members as you have in the past.

For a longer letter:

Some additional news is that <u>the Board met and agreed to option the</u>
(we voted to sell gift wrapping paper to raise money)

<u>land on Polk Street</u>.

Thank you again for your thoughtful support.

Nominations

The <u>treasurer's position</u> of <u>the Hampton Farm Homeowner's Association</u>
(cite position/the   *(cite organization)*
Steering Committee)

is an important position. I nominate <u>Trisha Locandro</u> to serve in this
(cite nominee)

key role. Trisha has <u>served our neighborhood as social chairman and</u>
*(organizational skills and an accounting background/
state what qualities or accomplishments distinguish your
candidate/you may want to write several paragraphs)*

<u>as a member of the board. She has worked on every event that has</u>

<u>successfully brought neighbors together</u>.

<u>Her</u> character, background, and skills make <u>her</u> the best choice for
(His)   *(him)*

this job.

Thank you for accepting my nomination.

VOLUNTEERING AND VOLUNTEERS

Asking for Volunteers

Do you have hopes that <u>the children of Cobb County will be safe and</u>
(the art of Cobb Country will be preserved)

<u>well cared for in the future?</u>

We do, too. Please join us as a volunteer as we work together

<u>to design a parent training program for underprivileged parents.</u>
(to raise money for a new wing for the Cobb Museum of Art)

You are especially valued as a volunteer because <u>you have demonstrated</u>
(of your Early Education
degree/of your knowledge
of contemporary art/of
your fundraising ability)

<u>your commitment to civic causes in the past.</u>

Please call me at (555) 666-7777 to confirm that you and I will be

working together as volunteers on this worthwhile project.

Volunteering

Your current <u>project</u> is of great interest to me. Please accept my offer
    (job/taskforce)

to help you as an enthusiastic volunteer. I want very much to work

on the Habitat for Humanity house.
(for the cause of the homeless/for the
Children's Academy Project)

I am especially interested because <u>the houses go to such deserving people.</u>
    (I believe our entire community benefits
    from this project/I would be honored to
    work for you/my wiring skills will be put
    to use on a very worthwhile project)

You will have many decisions to make in this <u>undertaking</u>. Please count
    (job)

on me to help you <u>in any way you choose.</u>
    (particularly in the area of
    typing and filing/to decorate)

Thank you for all that you do.

REQUESTS AND INVITATIONS

Asking for Sponsorship/Donations

You are being contacted because of your interest in the welfare of
*(civic and cultural improve-
ments in Cobb County/the
development of business in
our community)*

our children. With your help, the Civitan Club will be able to
*(Chamber of Commerce/
Social Committee)*

help fund the Milk for Lunch Program at area schools.
(build a sunroom at the high-rise for senior citizens)

Please join in the effort by agreeing to donate $500. I will be contacting
*(sponsor a fund-   (John Doe)
raising booth
for a fee of $100)*

you later this week for your answer. You are a neighbor whom we look
(member/local business)

to for support. We appreciate all you have done in the past. We hope

you see the value of supporting us in this new and important project.

To lend a hand to this worthy cause, simply send a check to John Doe.
(fun project)   *(sign the enclosed booth
application)*

Thank you again for being someone the children in need can look to
(who promotes local businesses)

for support.

Asking for the Loan of a Painting, Exhibit, or Historical Relic

Your decision to <u>purchase</u> the letters of General McLellan reflects both
(collect/ *(Menebonis print of Magnolias)*
acquire)

<u>wisdom</u> and a desire to invest in the future. Please invest in the future
(discrimination)

of <u>Cobb County</u> by agreeing to loan <u>these letters</u> for <u>a temporary exhibit.</u>
(our children/ *(this painting)* *(a week-long exhibit/*
Walker School) *our Fine Arts Day)*

The loan would be <u>from May 1–5, 2000</u>. You could <u>bring us the letters</u>
(only May 1st) *(trust our curator to*
transport and care
for your collection)

<u>yourself</u>. <u>The letters will be displayed in tamper-proof and humdity-</u>
(state how they will be cared for)

<u>controlled glass cases. A bonded messenger will pick up and transport</u>

<u>your letters for you.</u>

We have such admiration for your <u>collection</u>. Please consider sharing
(art works)

your marvelous <u>letters</u> with many who would appreciate <u>them</u>.
(prints) *(it)*

Inviting a Guest Speaker

Because of your <u>expertise in politics</u>, our <u>Rotary Club</u> extends this
        (renown in our community/   *(Administrative*
        popularity in our   *Department)*
        organization/recent
        experience in China)

invitation to you to speak at <u>our next breakfast</u>. We would be very
        (our September meeting/
        the Annual State Convention)

pleased if you agree to speak to our group. The details follow:

WHERE:	<u>Aztec Hotel, the Maya Room</u>
WHEN:	<u>8:00 A.M.</u>
	<u>Tuesday, May 15, 2000</u>
YOUR CONTACT:	<u>Jane Jenkins, Program Chairman</u>
	<u>(555) 666-7777</u>

Our group usually meets <u>for about thirty minutes</u> and the speaker
        (once a month)

speaks for <u>about 20–30 minutes</u>. Our group would be greatly interested
        (about an hour)

<u>in your addressing the recent legislation that affects property taxes</u>.
(in anything you choose as a topic)

To follow up, <u>I will call you in a few days</u>. I hope you will agree to share
        (please call me at (555) 777-6666)

your <u>thoughts</u> with our group. You will be a much-anticipated and
        (expertise)

much-appreciated speaker.

Thank you for considering this invitation from the <u>Canton Rotary Club</u>.

Invitation to Attend a Fundraising Event

How can you have a(n) <u>day</u> of fun, <u>save on your taxes</u>, and contribute
(evening)   (insert a benefit)

to <u>some special children at the same time</u>? Simply attend our
(the Church Building Fund)

<u>Third Annual Bass Fishing Contest to benefit St. James School for</u>
(Spring Fundraising Gala)

<u>Exceptional Children.</u>

Your entry fee is considered a charitable donation, one that offers you a tax benefit. How can you join us for this win/win event?

WHERE:	<u>Allatoona Lake</u>
	<u>Red Mountain Marina</u>
WHEN:	<u>June 17, 2000</u>
	<u>11:00 A.M.</u>
WHAT TO <u>BRING</u>:	<u>Your own bait and tackle;</u>
(wear/expect)	<u>We supply everything else for the day</u>

Many successes have been experienced by <u>the children who have been</u>
(the doctors doing this research)

<u>helped by your donations in past years</u>. Please help by joining us in this worthy cause.

RSVP to <u>Joan Hill, St. James Development Director, (555) 666-7777</u>.
(John Smith, Cobb Heart Association, (555) 777-6666)

CHAPTER
13

FORMATTING PERSONAL LETTERS

TIPS: Correct Formats for Personal Letters

•

Top Ten Guidelines for Formatting a Personal Letter

•

Top Ten Rules for Formatting a Personal Business Letter

•

Closings

•

TIPS: Closing Letters Effectively

- How can I format my personal letters to look polished and correct?

- What are today's guidelines for formatting personal letters?

TIPS: CORRECT FORMATS FOR PERSONAL LETTERS

First impressions really count in written correspondence. The way a letter initially strikes a reader colors how the person regards you, your message, and your requests. It's important to learn the right way to lay out a letter. These are items you may want to include, but you may be unsure of the correct format.

- Greetings

- Closings

- Spacing

- Your address

- Your reader's address

- Other items

These rules change, depending on whether you are writing a *Personal Letter* or a *Personal Business Letter.* The guidelines for both are detailed for you on the pages 189-190.

TOP TEN GUIDELINES FOR FORMATTING A PERSONAL LETTER

1. No need to include an inside address (yours or your reader's).

2. Put a comma after the salutation or greeting. Example: Dear Aunt Evelyn,

3. Include the date in the upper right-hand corner.

4. Use an informal but appropriate close:

Love,	Missing you,
Warmly,	Your friend,
Regards,	Fondly,
Highest regard,	Sincerely,

5. Always put a zip code. Your telephone book has local zips. Your library has out-of-state zips in the *National Zip Code Directory*.

6. Typing a personal letter is acceptable today.

7. Neatness counts:

   - Write legibly or type

   - Don't cram too much on a page. Use a second sheet of paper. Your reader wants to be able to read what you have written.

8. Use paper that suits your personality or occasion or use paper that suits the personality of the reader. The paper you use can add fun, dignity, or many other tones to your message.

9. Use your reader's first name in the greeting, if appropriate.

10. Enclosures can make a letter come alive. A few that I have seen put smiles on people's faces:

- Confetti
- Snapshots
- Children's drawings
- Ticket stubs
- Pressed flowers
- Four-leaf clovers

Personal Letter—Standard Format—Version One (May Be Typed or Handwritten)

May 4, 2000

Dear Jan,

You and I will soon be soaking up the sun at the beach. This is just a quick note to confirm that Houston and I will be arriving at your beach house on June 5. We should be in at around 6:00 P.M.

I can't wait!

Sincerely,

Personal Letter—Standard Format—Version Two (May Be Typed or Handwritten)

May 4, 2000

Dear Jan,

You and I will soon be soaking up the sun at the beach. This is just a quick note to confirm that Houston and I will be arriving at your beach house on June 5. We should be in at around 6:00 P.M.

I can't wait!

Sincerely,

TOP TEN RULES FOR FORMATTING A PERSONAL BUSINESS LETTER

1. Your address is included first, at the top of the page.

2. Today's date is beneath your address.

3. The address of the person to whom you are writing comes after the date.

4. Optionally, you may insert a line entitled "Subject"; "In Reference To"; or "Re:".

5. The salutation or greeting should be as specific as possible. Even if you have to call a company, find out the name of someone you can address your letter to, if possible. If that's not possible, still try to be as specific as possible:

   - Dear Board Members:
   - Dear Manager:
   - Dear Customer Service Supervisor:
   - Dear Faculty:

   If not, use one of the standards:

   - Dear Sir:
   - Dear Sir or Madam:
   - To Whom It May Concern:
   - Dear (name of company or department):

6. In the world of business, typed letters have greater power and credibility than do handwritten letters. If at all possible, type.

7. The body of the paragraph should be only as long as it needs to be:

    - Short and to the point

    - Complete with all information the reader needs to take care of your business for you. Don't leave out vital facts that the reader may need for tracking or support.

8. The closing should be appropriate to the reader and situation. "Sincerely" is my favorite, but here are others:

    - Cordially,

    - With great interest,

    - Best regards,

    - Concerned,

9. Always include the complete address. Do not leave out the following:

    - Any department or location information within a company or organization. Find out if the reader has a mail code or BIN number within the company.

    - Zip code (use the telephone book or *National Zip Code Directory* at the library).

10. Use white or near white, neutral-colored paper. Create a businesslike first impression of yourself by making a statement with your paper.

The appearance of your letter makes a statement. An off-white paper with black ink and matching envelope says, "I am a credible person who knows what I'm talking about." A letter written on pink paper with gray kittens and stuffed in a nonmatching envelope says, "I'm a lightweight. You don't need to take me or my request seriously."

Layout of a Personal Business Letter—Version One

6990 Trailside Drive
Marietta, GA 30064
April 19, 2000

Mr. James Ford, C.P.A.
President *(title)*
Ford and Ford Accounting Group
1000 Ansley Drive
Atlanta, GA 30342

Dear Mr. Ford: ← *(colon)*

　　Your help was so valuable in settling my grandmother's estate. I am writing to request that you act once more on my behalf. Please send my <u>brother</u>

(name)

a copy of the plan you gave me for investing the money for the family trust. His address is as follows:

　　Name
　　4973 Ivy Court
　　Buckhead, GA 30327

　　Again, I am grateful for the time and sensitivity you have shown in this matter.

Sincerely, ← *(Close)*

← *4 spaces*

Jane Doe ← *(Handwritten signature)*

Jane Doe ← *(Type or print)*

195

Today's Choice—Modified Block Style

Many successful letter writers today prefer modified block style. Everything is aligned to the left margin except the writer's inside address. You do not indent the first five spaces of every paragraph. Business letters first adopted this style. More and more, we are seeing this style in personal letters.

Why is this method preferred? Your lists, tables, and vital information stand out more dramatically and clearly in modified block style. An example of the modified block style is on the following page.

Personal Business Letter–
Version Two

6990 Trailside Drive
Marietta, GA 30064

April 19, 2000

spaces ➤

Mr. James Ford, C.P.A.
President *(title)*
Ford and Ford Accounting Group
1000 Ansley Drive
Atlanta, GA 30342

2 spaces ➤

Dear Mr. Ford: ← *(colon)*

1 space ➤

Your help was so valuable in settling my grandmother's estate. I am writing to request that you act once
more on my behalf. Please send my <u>brother</u> a copy of
                                      (name)
the plan you gave me for investing the money for the
family trust. His address is as follows:

> Name
> 4973 Ivy Court
> Buckhead, Georgia 30327

Again, I am grateful for the time and sensitivity you
have shown in this matter.

Sincerely,   ← *(Close)*

                              ← *4 spaces*

Jane Doe   ← *(Handwritten signature)*
Jane Doe   ← *(Type or print)*

CLOSINGS

How appropriate that the closing chapter of this book should be about closing remarks. We are discussing here the last sentence(s) in the body, not the complimentary closing such as "Sincerely" or "Love." A good closing is almost as important as a great first line in a letter. Why?

- Closings leave an impression of the writer
- Closings leave an impression on the reader

You end a letter with a certain tone, based on your closing. Your tone may be positive or negative; cooperative or intimidating; admiring or unfeeling.

Some surveys show that, second to the opening line, the closing line of a letter is the most powerful line you will write. The following are some TIPS for writing a strong closing.

TIPS: CLOSING LETTERS EFFECTIVELY

1. <u>End on a high note</u>. Even if you have written a letter of complaint, end with a tone that says you have confidence that the reader will respond positively to your letter.

   <u>Examples:</u>

   - I look forward to seeing the improvements you will make

   - Thank you for stepping in and handling this for me

   - Going forward, I'm sure you will have great success

2. <u>Keep it brief</u>. Don't feel the need to summarize what you said in the letter.

3. <u>If appropriate, include a compliment to the reader or the reader's organization</u>. Some trite sayings are valid: you do "catch more flies with honey than with vinegar." A simple, unelaborate compliment in the closing often warms your reader's heart and gets you the response that you want.

   <u>Examples:</u>

   - We have long admired The Westminster Schools and appreciate the opportunity to submit Johnny's application for enrollment in 2001.

   - Your store's long history of excellent services makes me confident you will resolve this problem satisfactorily.

   - With your stellar academic record, you should do well long after graduation.

4. <u>Focus on the next step</u>. If you have asked for something, make sure your statement prompts the reader to take action.

Examples:

- Although I appreciate how busy you are, I look forward to hearing your suggestions soon.

- I'd be grateful if you'd furnish the forms to me soon so that I can return them to you promptly.

- Because we are excited about the prospect of attending your popular seminar, we hope that you will send the applications to us right away.

In closing, one more point must be made. Be sincere. Although you can polish your language and your style by reviewing the examples, be sure to be yourself.

- Choose words that you feel comfortable using.

- Experiment. Phrase your sentences different ways until it sounds like "you."

If you make these efforts for your reader's gratification, you will be gratified by the response you are sure to receive.